THE ZOO

Eric Robson

Bookcase

Copyright Eric Robson 2007
ISBN 978-1-904147-26-8
First edition
Published by Bookcase
19 Castle Street, Carlisle, CA3 8SY
01228 544560 bookcasecarlisle@aol.com

CHAPTER ONE

'It's the wrong bloody way up....'

Pike stopped fighting with the chaos of rope at the bottom of the flagpole and raised his eyes to a deep blue heaven.

'... or the wrong bloody way round.'

Pike's head sank.

'In fact are you sure it's not the wrong bloody flag?'

Henry Jardine wasn't having a good morning. It was hot. It was Ship Day and he hated Ship Day. He was sure this was going to be a particularly stressful Ship Day. To make matters worse he'd drunk altogether too much at the Joint Staffs party the previous night and his stomach was playing up.

'It did come out of Area 14's safe,' Pike snapped. 'And the bag I took it out of said FORMERLY UGANDA. Anything else you'd like me to check....' Pike glowered in the direction of his tormentor. '...Sir?'

Jardine was a slight, dapper man. His shock of white hair, falling to his shoulders seemed rather too bohemian; at odds with his general air of precision. He pulled himself up to his full five feet six and fixed the younger man with a piercing stare. 'As you're so bloody efficient, Mr. Pike, you'll no doubt remember with ease the incident of the Liberian National Anthem, except it was the Congolese National Anthem wasn't it?' Jardine turned on his heel and immediately felt dizzy and rather queasy. To make matters worse he was almost bowled over by the red carpet being rolled down the sloping quay by a couple of dock workers.

'Look at the state of it? It looks as if you've been keeping bloody seagulls in it? Get it hoovered. Get it hoovered NOW.' Jardine somehow managed to sidestep the advancing roll and headed for the matronly comfort of the Rolls Royce's deep leather seats. It was parked beside an empty polished granite plinth. Jardine glanced up at it as he drove away and groaned again, partly because of his dancing stomach, but mainly because it reminded him he still had to organise getting the bloody statue from the warehouse.

Pike watched the ancient black and yellow car slowly disappearing up the main street and fervently hoped Sir Henry's hangover was a symptom of something terminal.

***

Lady Jardine watched the car approaching from her bedroom window in Government House. Her hangover was under rather better control mainly by reason of the fact that she had a large Bloody Mary chinking in an unsteady hand, but helped by the attentions of Momo who'd been summoned from the butler's pantry to take her mind off it. For some reason he also seemed to have mislaid the bottom half of his uniform. Had Sir Henry entered the room at that precise moment Momo would undoubtedly have found himself on a charge because H.E. was a stickler for proper dress.

'Better… put a spurt on, Momo. Judging by the speed Sir Henry's driving you've got about…..four…. minutes.'

Momo went into a brief overdrive and her ladyship bounced alarmingly almost, but not quite, spilling her drink as she filled her mouth with ice cubes to stifle the ladylike yelp. Ethne Jardine had always prided herself on her timing – years of organising Embassy soirees – and the hangover treatment was completed with the unhurried efficiency of Royal Ceremonial. The back of the Hardy Amies was smoothed down, an errant wisp of grey hair had been put back in position and Momo had just packed himself into his tight and pressed trousers when the door crashed open and Henry Jardine barged into the room.

'Bloody Pike, I'm sure he's got the wrong flag again.'

Momo snapped to attention as Sir Henry threw his panama in the vague direction of a sofa and pointed at the butler's trousers.

'And how many times do I have to tell you Momo that your belt buckle has to be *precisely* in the centre not somewhere in the vicinity of the centre. Just like Pike you're neither use nor bloody ornament.'

'A drink dear?'

Ethne smiled and took Henry's arm in case he decided to make a closer inspection of Momo's subsiding accoutrements.

'And you have to be nice to Momo today, dear, because he's probably a little nervous.'

'What's he got to be nervous about? It's me that's got to stand on the pier and be made a laughing stock by incompetents who don't know the difference between the Star and Garter and the Star Spangled bloody Banner.'

'Because it's a special Ship Day for him, dear. As they used to say in the old song –*some day my prince will come*,' she trilled as she poured a large scotch and soda.

'Ah,' said Henry, the significance of Ethne's point slowly creeping through the fog and being brought into focus by the Black Label. 'Which means….'

'Yes, dear.'

'Which means… that he knows what the bloody Ugandan flag looks like.'

Ethne Jardine beamed into her glass, realising once again, as she so often did, that she was a worthy member of that heavenly host of diplomatic wives who had ever been and continued to be the real power of the Empire.

Momo for his part decided not to mention that, though he was black and though he was African, having spent most of his life in Brixton, he knew as much about Uganda as Sir Henry knew about hangover cures.

' Splendid," said Sir Henry, subsiding into an armchair. 'Get yourself down to the pier and check that it's the Ugandan flag that's up the bloody pole because with Pike in charge we're just as likely to be up the bloody spout.'

***

Donald Reeves, the American Ambassador, had been having a more relaxing start to the day than either Henry or Ethne Jardine.

Dressed in nothing but tight and tiny Lycra shorts and a pair of gleaming cowboy boots he was taking a leisurely ride on his exercise bike and admiring his tanned physique in the mirror that filled almost the whole of one wall. His study in the modern Embassy building had views over Jamestown Roads and he could see the last minute arrangements raging on the quay. He enjoyed British Ship Days because they usually made such a hog's breakfast of them. Which, of course, made it so much easier when it came round to the American turn. That and the fact the Americans knew amateurism was a sin rather than the art form the British believed it to be.

The telephone rang. As he reached to answer it he looked out across the harbour and over the wide expanses of the Atlantic beyond. On days like today, he thought, there couldn't be a more pleasant posting.

'Reeves…'

At which point his day suddenly got worse.

'Goddam it they all know it's Ship Day and there's been a multilateral for years that Ship Day's a dispute-free zone.'

On British Ship Days the Americans were in sole charge of colonial security and Ambassador Reeves suddenly saw the British de-briefing cocktail party (which he had to concede they organised surprisingly well) disappearing under a pile of reports and recriminations.

'Well send Schwartz and his peace keeping squad up there to sort it.'

The American Ambassador's exercise bike ground to a halt.

'What do you mean they've been taken into protective custody? It's us who do pro-tective custody, not the fucking Liberians.'

He dismounted as if from a galloping palomino and, telephone tucked under his squared chin, quickly turned to the appropriate section of *Federation Rules*, a thick volume emblazoned with eagle and crown that sat in the middle of his otherwise empty desk. He scanned the clauses – negotiation, extenuation, proscribed response, punishment and said

'Send the goddam tank.'

***

The warehouse which had once been a flax store (and, briefly, the execution hall of the Jamestown prison) before it was requisitioned by The Powers, was dusty and cobwebbed. Shafts of light came through rusting holes in the corrugated iron roof touching, here and there, a shadowy face, a horse's head, a grand uniform in bronze, a clenched fist in stone. The place had the air of a long forgotten Madame Tussaud's except that here the statues generally resembled the people they were supposed to represent. With a screech of grit trapped in rusted rollers the metal doors were hauled open and the moted morning sunlight fell on the once great and the not so good.

Sir Henry had come to personally supervise the moving of the statue. Having sent Momo to sort out the flag he was feeling rather more chipper about the afternoon's events and once the plinth was filled there would just be the garrison band and Major Clarkson's inappropriately named Guard of Honour to be given a talking to. As the doors ground apart Jardine marched into the swirling cloud of dancing dust particles. Florence Lacey, The Keeper of the Regalia, laden down with files, strolled along behind. She was taller than Sir Henry and broader. Her deep voice, gravelled by forty cigarettes a day, echoed round the shed.

'He's in bay 42, Sir Henry, and we've already had him cleaned down because he's been in store for almost fifteen years you know. Doesn't time fly when the world's having fun?'

'And no doubt there are five or six parked in front of him if the organisation's up to its usual standard,' said Jardine as he strode on between an equestrian monstrosity and a giant officer's boot on the neck of a fallen soldier. The rest of the general disappeared up into the warehouse shadows.

'We did have a small problem with the fork lift truck,' Florence boomed, 'but you'll be pleased to hear that it's been sorted out, Sir Henry.'

"Pleased, Miss Lacey?" Sir Henry looked over his half spectacles and drew himself up to his full, bristling five feet six.

'Why on earth should I be pleased? Correct me if I'm wrong, but I was under the impression we were trying to run a Colony here, not a bloody plant hire firm.'

They were walking into Africa through dark tunnels between the statues. Here the Sultan of Zanzibar; there Chief Dinizulu; left past General Cronje, hero of the Boers.

'And here he is.'

From the larger than life polished boots the impeccable bronze uniform rose fifteen feet to a broad expanse of chest, heavy with medals. The face was in deep shadow under the peak of a square set cap.

'We wouldn't want to get on his wrong side, would we,' said Florence, looking up into the gloom, as they heard a roar of throaty engine from beyond the warehouse door. Jardine looked puzzled.

'Just the forklift,' said Florence cheerily, flicking through her papers trying to find the correct form for Jardine to sign to release the statue for duty. 'I told you they'd fixed it.'

'That's not the forklift. It's the bloody tank. What's Reeves doing with the bloody tank? Give him security for one day and he's off playing bloody war games again.'

***

Colin Shwartz and his peace keepers were having a precarious ride along rutted roads on Horse Ridge over the Liberian border. The battered Mitsubishi pick up bucked through potholes between banks of prickly pear while their beaming and trigger happy captors celebrated by firing their Kalashnikovs into the trees. Shwartz wasn't sure who was more spooked, himself or the flocks of wire birds hugging the ground and dodging the bullets.

'No worries Swartzboss,' shouted Tasawe over the roar of the failing exhaust, 'we going celebration party.' Judging by the smell of his breath it would be his second party of the day. 'And you going be entainment dancy dancy.'

'You realise you're in deep shit, Tassy.' Shwartz shouted back to the man in the filthy Black Sabbath tee shirt. 'This is a friggin hanging offence.'

'Gotta catch us fore they hang us.' He flashed black toothy stumps. 'An we got the spirit of leebaration upon us.'

'You'll all be gettin leeberated from this goddam planet when Reeves gets his hands on your ass.'

'Well now, Swartzy, we might just vite ol cowboy to the party as well.' A cackle and another burst of gunfire as the pick- up raised a billowing cloud of red dust through a shanty town of cabins with sagging roofs and termite eaten verandahs.

'Does Chuckie know about this?'

'Now you know well as me, he knows evertin goin on in his country.'

The pick up skidded to a halt by a group of army tents set up in the shade of a clump of trees. Tasawe indicated with a twitch of the gun for Shwartz and his peacekeepers to climb out.

'Anyhow, no need to deal widde greasy rag, ask him youself Missa Shwartz.'

From one of the tents emerged a saintly vision, the spit of Martin Luther King dressed in a full length white robe. They'd apparently been granted an audience with the big boss - Charles Taylor, preacher and part time war criminal, saviour of his people and occasionally murderous President of the Republic of Liberia.

Shwartz stood up in the back of the truck. 'President Taylor, on behalf of the administration of the United States of America I pro-test about this criminality.'

Taylor raised his hands in beatific welcome but then looked sternly at his reluctant little congregation through half closed eyes. 'Jesus Christ, too, was accused of being a criminal in his time.'

'Oh shit, he'sn Christian mood. An dat's reely nasty,' whispered Tasawe behind Shwartz' shoulder. 'Welcome to de croosifixtion party.'

***

Four days out of Capetown Her Majesty's frigate Northumberland rolled in a lazy sea off Sugarloaf Point. From his vantage point on the wing bridge Captain Macdiarmid was watching rehearsals on deck. He really didn't like being a bus driver, however important the passengers. And the passenger on this trip was being particularly difficult. He leaned on the Tannoy switch and his voice echoed round the ship. 'Do try to make it look like the *British* navy, Mr Johnston.' After a spate of bellowing, the lining party shuffled into a straighter line. 'And the cage needs to be closer to the companionway, Mr. Johnston, unless you're expecting the President to skate board off the ship.' Macdiarmid shook his head. But at least tomorrow they'd be on their way to proper duties patrolling the Falklands.

To port, the sheer cliffs of the Colony rose out of a line of surf. Here and there tiny white houses seemed to have been glued to them. Through his binoculars the Captain could see an occasional grander bungalow set in terraced gardens on the higher mountain slopes. Between them and the sea cliffs the landscape was a forbidding scrubland of red earth and cactus interspersed with ridges of sub tropical vegetation. The bridge intercom squawked.

'Yes.'

'Valet, sir. He's refusing to get dressed, sir.' Shouts and clatters in the background almost drowned him out.

'Well he's refused to do anything else he's been told on this trip so why should that surprise us.'

'Because he's strutting about stark naked, shouting and waving his regalia in the air and scaring the ratings, sir, and he says he's going ashore like that so his people can see their master in all his glory.'

'And is he scaring you or just putting you to shame?'

'Let's just say it was a wise decision of yours to ban the Wrens from this deck, Sir. We wouldn't want a rash of suicidal boyfriends, would we, sir?'

Macdiarmid strolled down to D deck where two Royal Marines sentries stood guard at the door of the secure accommodation. It sounded as if Rorke's Drift was being re-enacted inside. He unlocked the door and stepped into the cabin which turned out to look not so much like a battle scene on the veldt, more an explosion in a laundry. Uniforms were scattered on every surface. The valet was half in and half out of the wardrobe and a powerfully built black figure, entirely naked but for an officer's cap and gleaming with exertion, was trying to close the door.

'And a very good morning to you Mr. President,' said Macdiarmid.

The man turned and the captain couldn't fail to notice that he was obviously finding the dispute ennervating.

'Ah, my Admiral, comn sense has been rived.' As the valet slumped to the wardrobe floor the man walked forward and grasped Macdiarmid in a powerful embrace.

'I'm sure this infringes any number of lower decks rules, Mr. President,' said the captain, extricating himself from the sweaty display of affection. 'I believe you're not happy with the uniform for today's ceremony.'

'Prison unform, Captain. Madjacket whiffing Imperial stink.'

'It looks a very handsome uniform to me,' said Macdiarmid, picking up a Field Marshal's jacket from the floor. 'And so many medals. But of course your heroism is legendary, Mr. President.'

'No more tan should be spected from great leader. Tree Veectoria Crosses. No one in damn world has more.'

Macdiarmid chinked the cash and carry VCs and ran his thumb over the home made Garter Star. 'Such a pity your people won't be able to see them today.'

'My people will see tem. I deeecree it.'

'And I'm most happy to bow to your command, Mr. President, but you can scarcely go ashore with them tied round your neck on a bit of string.... or dangling from your dick for that matter. So do stop being a Presidential nuisance and get into the damned uniform. Sir.' He swung on his heel and walked out. Mr. President, his head cocked to one side, looked again at the medals and slowly began to get dressed.

***

On the harbourside the men of Major Harding's Honour Guard were mooching about waiting for the inevitable dressing down from Ambassador Jardine but grateful that the band had made such a hash of the National Anthem that Sir Henry was tiring himself out on them first.

'Have these men ever SEEN these instruments before, let alone practiced with them, bandmaster? I've heard better on the bloody Eurovision Song Contest.'

They staggered into another rendering and, after twenty seconds or so, had more or less all caught up. Meanwhile Pike, head and shoulders taller than anyone else on the quayside, gangled about in a crumpled linen suit organising the crowd scenes, trying to persuade the people with the darkest faces to stand at the front under a limp banner that proclaimed WELCOME HOME PRESIDENT FOR LIFE AND SAVIOUR OF OUR NATION. There was a time when the banners were more specific but the Joint Staffs had decided on one size fits all during one of the regular spasms of economy ordered by London and Washington.

'If that was the first thing I heard when I got here I'd refuse to get off the bloody ship,' Sir Henry shouted and the band subsided into merciful silence. 'In fact it probably infringes several clauses of the United Nations Charter on Human Rights.'

The basilisk eye turned to Major Harding who brought his men to what passed for attention on either side of the statue which had been safely installed on the plinth under Florence's direction.

'Major Harding, so dreadfully sorry to trouble you but just in the interests of us all singing from the same hymn sheet may I be so bold as to point out that this is supposed to be a Presidential welcome not the official opening of a bloody fish and chip shop in Barnsley. So for the next couple of hours might it just be possible to persuade your inadequately dressed rabble to PRETEND, I don't ask for much - pretence will do, to PRETEND that on a far off occasion in a distant land they'd actually seen, if not experienced, the challenges of a bloody parade ground.'

'We need more children to look adoring down here at the front,' shouted Pike over the renewed scuffings and shufflings of the Honour Guard "and where's the cushion with the State Crown?'

'On the back seat of Sir Henry's car, Florence called down from the fork lift prongs which had raised her to put a bright garland of flowers round the statue's neck.

Sir Henry, meanwhile, stood fanning himself with his panama at the edge of the quay, looked back at the assembled cast of the ceremonial about to unfold and saw that it was as tatty as it was possible to be without the involvement of the D'Oyly Carte Company. If they got through it without a major cock up it would be a bloody miracle.

***

The radio in the American Embassy incident room crackled with pulsing interference as Donald Reeves ran a finger across the Colony map to the Liberian border. He knew Jardine would take a dim view of him sending in the tank–cowboys and bloody indians he'd call it. But Reeves didn't like trouble from the natives. If Chuckie Taylor wanted a last stand he was happy to oblige and Jardine could go play with his protocols.

Radio traffic occasionally cut through the static keeping Reeves in touch with the progress of the Abraham as it trundled out along dirt roads at the head of Thompson Valley and approached the Liberian frontier crossing.

'Barriers down.... Barriers gone...'

Reeves imagined the matchwood the tank had made of the Liberian frontier post, stabbed the air and shouted 'Yessir' to the Stars and Stripes draped photograph of the beaming President which had pride of place behind his desk. 'We'll show a bunch of cotton pickin' troublemakers who's boss, Mr. President.'

Another break in the static.

'We got a praablem...'

He jammed a manicured finger onto the answer key. 'What problem?'

A long burst of radio hiss blotted out the reply.

'What problem for Chrissakes...?' The pink was showing through Reeves' tan and his blonde crew cut seemed to be standing even more sharply to attention.

'A Lady Ethne praablem... she's, eh....' There was a long pause broken only by electronic twitterings. '...She's, eh.....'

'She's eh what?'

'She's, eh...standing in front of the tank and refuses to get outta the damned way.' The last bit spoken all of a rush by the obviously embarrassed radio operator.

Tempted as he was to order the tank commander to drive on regardless, Reeves couldn't help but think of the snowstorm of reports that would blow up in the wake of any order to leave tank tracks up the front of the British Ambassador's wife.

'What's her problem?'

More hissing and breakup during which Reeves remembered it was Jardine's British bosses who'd refused to spend the money to upgrade the comms. network.

'She says she wants to talk to you Mr. Aambassador.'

Lady Ethne's trill cut through the crackle. 'I insist that this silliness stops immediately, Ambassador Reeves.'

'Now, listen here Lady Ethne....'

'No, listen THERE Mr. Reeves. Simply because you're God Bless American does not give you the right to practice armed aggression against Sovereign States without the express approval of the Joint Powers and as Sir Henry is otherwise engaged this morning, which you well know, obviously no such negotiation has taken place....'

'But you don't...'

'But nothing, Mr Reeves. Not only are you in breach of International law and Colonial standing orders but this morning you are jeopardising our long planned charitable mission to the Republic of Liberia. As I speak the ladies of the Anglo Liberian aid society are parked in front of your tank with cars full of clothes and medicines donated by good people in England which we have every intention of delivering to the school in Monrovia as planned...'

'Lady Ethne...'

'And charity tends to lose its charm when crushed under the tracks of a battle tank, don't you agree, Ambassador..?'

14

'Lady Ethne...' Reeves was shouting now. "We have a code red here...'

'Do please try to speak in English rather than Pentagonic gobbledegook, Mr Reeves, and may I be permitted to point out that I have no problems whatsoever with my hearing so it's entirely unnecessary to shout.'

'Lady Ethne we've lost a whole peace keeping team.'

'Well that's extremely careless of you, Ambassador,' said Lady Ethne.

Reeves tried to re-establish some semblance of authority while at the same time trying to put from his mind the image of an impeccably dressed middle aged English lady in sensible shoes standing astride his tank turret. And worse, the tank's crew rolled about in fits of laughter.

'They've been AB-DUCTED Lady Ethne and I have no goddam alternative but send the tank to get them back.'

'I've always felt that blasphemy and diplomacy were uncomfortable bedfellows, Ambassador and there's obviously some quite simple misunderstanding which I will take up with President Taylor presently. In the meantime Mrs Butler and Mrs Armitage have volunteered to position themselves fore and aft to ensure there's no further silliness. Good morning, Mr Reeves.....'

The line went dead.

***

HMS Northumberland lay at Anchor in Jamestown bay. Porpoises rose in the shadow of the grey hull. At noon precisely the lining party came to attention and Captain Macdiarmid walked out on deck a few paces ahead of an imposing figure in Field Marshal's uniform. They stepped into a grey metal cage, an officer closed the safety gate and the ship's forward derrick lifted them effortlessly over the rail and deposited them amidships in the British lighter. It pulled out of the shadow of the frigate, the Royal Standard fluttering red, blue and gold at the stern and turned towards the quay.

Pike, now sweltering in a heavy embroidered robe and full

bottomed wig and carrying a crown on a purple velvet cushion hissed at Major Harding, who looked for all the world as if he'd nodded off. He started, gave an order and the Honour guard tentatively shouldered then presented arms. Florence Lacey encouraged the crowd under the banner to break into desultory cheering and waving.

When the lighter came alongside, a clattering dockside crane hooked up the cage and lifted it gently onto the quay at the end of the red carpet. As it touched dry land the band struck up the National Anthem. Captain Macdiarmid opened the metal gate and saluted as the Field Marshal stepped out, sunlight shimmering from his expanse of medals.

So far so bloody good, thought Sir Henry as he stood by Pike's left shoulder dressed in black frock coat and plumed hat. The white feathers moved gently in a welcome breeze from the sea as the band wheezed to a halt and the Ambassador stepped forward.

'Mr President, on behalf of Her Most Gracious Majesty I welcome you home. As you can see, your people rejoice in your return.'

The band made a rather shaky attempt at a fanfare as Sir Henry stood on tiptoe, and even then only just able to reach, replaced the President's Field Marshal's cap with the Crown of State. The sun shattered through it into reds and emeralds that danced about the quay as the Ambassador turned, took a manuscript scroll from the dripping Pike and read the tribute.

'Most High. Lord of all the beasts of the earth and fishes of the sea. Conqueror of the British Empire in Africa. King of Scotland. Life President of Uganda. Idi Amin Dada Oumee. Your loyal people salute you.'

Another strangled fanfare as Sir Henry turned on his heel and led the way through the parted crowd to the old black and yellow Rolls Royce. Momo, now dressed as chauffeur, held open the door as the President beamed down on his people and waved a hand of thick fingers as if he was stirring the heavy air.

'Children of Ooganda.' Said the President in a surprisingly

mellow voice as he threw his arms wide casting a larger than life crucifix shadow across the crowd, 'Daddy bin come home pronto way.' A solitary, piping cheer came from a little dusty boy in the shadow. Amin beamed over him. 'Suffer deeece lil kidlings.' And he reached down and lofted the startled boy to his pursed lips. Jardine couldn't help remembering the party-piece story one British diplomat used to tell about Amin.

'They say he loves children, don't you know, but they're a bit vague about how many he has at a sitting.' Always got a laugh at Embassy receptions but perhaps better not try it now.

As the President bent his crowned six feet four to set the trembling little boy back on the quay his eyes were suddenly level with Jardine's.

'Send which man put upside down flag see me.'

Big Daddy was back.

CHAPTER TWO

The Prime Minister's official spokesman was having a problem breathing having jogged into work from the far reaches of darkest Islington. As he overtook John Prescott on the stairs of Number Ten, the slow moving Honourable Member for Hull fish quay chuckled and suggested the gasper should trade in his pager for a pacemaker.

On the first floor landing Prime Minister Blair was deep in conversation with his Foreign Secretary who, despite recent press reports, was not rolling on his back with his legs in the air waiting for his master to tickle his stomach. Instead he was pointing out a small paragraph at the bottom of page twelve in the Daily Telegraph with the headline REBEL ATTACK IN LIBERIA.

'No change there, then,' grunted Prescott as he arrived on the landing and peered over the reader's shoulder. This casual foray into foreign affairs prompted an unstatesmanlike grimace from the Foreign Secretary.

'You really ought to know John, if you could find time to squeeze in the odd cabinet briefing between black pudding breakfasts and meetings of the Jaguar owners' club, that there *isn't* a Liberia anymore. It's part of the Joint Powers Western Africa Federation.'

'So who's making trouble?' asked Blair sourly having not yet got round to fitting his public smile for the day.

'It'll be the bastards in the CIA,' Alistair Campbell managed to get out as he gasped for breath on the landing with his hands on his knees. 'They've got more part time reporters on their payroll than spooks these days.'

'But the really concerning thing,' said the Foreign Secretary, looking down on Campbell as if he was something that had just crawled from under the skirting boards, 'there really *is* a spot of bother in the Liberian Colony.'

'And what's the Liberian Colony when it's at home with its assegai up its jaxi?' asked Prescott.

'Not part of your Ministerial brief, John,' said the Foreign Secretary in a tone that suggested he wouldn't understand even if it was. 'But I've managed to get some details of the incident, Prime Minister, and I understand the American Ambassador has the affair under control.'

Prescott made a mental note to find out a bit more about the Liberian Colony and another to find a way of wiping the sneer from the Foreign Secretary's supercilious mug. But in the meantime he concentrated on making sure the door of the cabinet room slammed shut just as his high and mightiness tried to glide through it

***

The Rolls Royce was labouring on the steep road out of Jamestown and Sir Henry was relishing the thought of sending Pike across to Kampala as a lunchtime snack for the President. Idi Amin, who'd been shouting meaningless instructions to Momo, glowered out of the window at the struggle of poor houses lining the track and lurched sideways into the Ambassador as the car's springs complained through a particularly deep pothole.

'Place clapped up.'

Sir Henry couldn't, in truth, disagree but to the best of his knowledge Jamestown had always been bloody well clapped up; had probably been built clapped up. If Amin thought the place had gone downhill he was certainly thinking of somewhere else. As indeed he had to be.

'How British made this Empire thing past my brain I tinking...'

The car lumbered round the hairpin that doubled out to Ladder Hill and to the west Sir Henry could see HMS Northumberland escaping to the open sea. He rather wished he was on board. He caught a reflection of Amin in the window and noted that, despite the president's 70 odd years, he was still strong and fit. The bulk wasn't fat. Stories about his passion for weight training and the three miles he swam every day during his exile in Jeddah may indeed have been true. Mind you getting out of Uganda again would put his bloody swimming skills to the test, he thought. Sir Henry allowed himself a flicker of a smile as the car climbed out above Jamestown, its houses hemmed in below them by walls of dirty rock.

'Car clapped up. Why you people not send Presdent's car?'

'I think your sports car might have struggled with the state of the roads, President.'

'Not with Africa rally champ in wheel,' Amin chuckled and Sir Henry remembered his passenger had become rally champion of Uganda by reason of the fact that the other competitors had sufficient survival instinct to pull over, feign breakdown and let the black Toad of Toad Hall past in a cloud of dust. He wasn't sure if the Presidential Mercedes did anything quite so common as 'toot, toot' but with Idi Amin's foot on the accelerator it probably did.

'If Mercedes not safe and shine Liz getting another sharpish you hear mister excellency.' This accompanied by a playful but painful dig in the Ambassador's ribs.

Amin's bizarre requests and demands of Her Majesty had kept the children of many an inadequate stand up comic in shoes through the years of the President's exile.

'I'm sure Her Majesty's Government will ensure you have the tools to do the job, Mr. President.'

And hopefully it would take some weeks for Amin to notice that the Mercedes no longer existed having been pressed into service as a barbecue by an ungrateful Ugandan rebel some years earlier.

As if reading the Ambassador's mind.

'Time for a bit of slapping his dash. Cat away too long mister. Mice been hokey cokey.' Amin brought his great hands together like a set of man trap jaws. Sir Henry looked into the bulging and yellowed eyes and remembered that Amin once told a reporter he couldn't possibly be a cannibal because he found human flesh too salty. Oh, yes, there were going to be fun and games now.

***

'Leg or breast, Lady Jardine? Charles Taylor spoke with a soft

American accent, a legacy of studying economics for three years at College in Massachusetts and then, in place of a PHD, doing fifteen months for embezzlement in the Massachusetts County Jail. Two waiters, perhaps ten or twelve years old and wearing startling blonde afro wigs, stood beside his chair with salvers of scrawny chicken pieces. Lady Ethne crooked a finger, swished away the flies and selected a particularly small morsel from each salver. She beamed at the President as if welcoming the vicar to a summer fete or being hostess at the cricket tea. Taylor clapped once and the semi circle of barefoot and bewigged children at his feet cheered and shuffled in the dust. A casual observer may have deduced they'd raided a fancy dress hamper, draped as they were in hand-me-down collarless shirts and tweed waistcoats with a scattering of crumpled cocktail frocks and ruched blouses. Gifts from Middle England.

'But I understand that on this lovely day, when the good people of Britain are offering the hand of international friendship, there's just the tiniest of black clouds on the horizon, Mr. President?"

'Surely not. Nothing must be allowed to intrude on our celebrations, Lady Ethne. And certainly not a *black* cloud.' He turned slowly to look her full in the face and smiled a set of expensive teeth. Another clap. Another half hearted cheer.

Lady Ethne leaned closer. 'Peace keepers, President Taylor. Mislaid peace keepers.'

'Careless.'

'Strangely, I said that myself not an hour ago. But there's also been a spot of shooting, I understand.'

'High spirits and boredom. Nothing more.'

'The Americans see it rather differently, I fear.'

'Ah, but the Americans still think of we Liberians as poor slaves to be patronised, dear lady. Do you know Reagan once called me 'boy' to my face?'

'He was a bad enough actor with a script, Charles. Unfortunately Nancy encouraged him to believe he had a talent for ad-libbing.' Lady Ethne shuddered at the thought of the awful Nancy and her lack of breeding. Charles Taylor she liked much better, despite his dreadful reputation. He had charm and, as she often used to say to Sir Henry, charm makes up for such a lot because people with charm can generally be persuaded. Given time.

The child army had grown restive round the President's feet and he shooed them away before leaning in towards Lady Ethne. 'And as you'll remember I have a particular distaste for peacekeepers, Lady Jardine, after that unseemly business with the Americans and the Nigerians.' His eyes flashed.

'Judas the peacekeeper.' He whispered, his mouth just a couple of inches from Lady Ethne's ear. A reference to the unlikely alliance of American and Nigerian peace keeping forces that had sent Charles Taylor into exile from Liberia not so many years before.

'Bygones, Mr. President. We must let them be. And, much as you and I may dislike certain American, how shall we put it ..attitudes… as I recall they did at least play a part in flummoxing the busybodies at the International War Crimes Commission.' She looked at him with a raised eyebrow.

He cocked an eyebrow in return. 'Ah, beware those creatures who live in the grey area between the winners and the losers, Lady Ethne. Yea though I dwell in the valley of the shadow of death I fear no evil.' Charles Taylor had a habit of speaking in inscribed antimacassars.

'Quite. But having put away childish things what we must surely concentrate on now is the business of good government, Mr President.'

Taylor stood and looked out from the compound into the heart of his country. 'You know my boys believe those wigs they're wearing will protect them even from bullets. Superstition, if properly harnessed, can be very useful.' He smiled down at her. 'But I have an even more powerful shield. The Lord himself stands between me and my enemies.' Lady Jardine was uncharacteristically stumped for a reply.

Taylor stood for some moments looking to the broad skies then shook himself back to more mundane considerations. 'Sadly, government needs money and good government needs big money. If

22

I can't pay my soldiers I have very little control over what they do and a hungry mercenary – particularly one protected by a magic wig – can at times be a troublesome creature.'

'As you know, Charles, Sir Henry takes a dim view of blackmail. Brings back unhappy memories of dealings with the whips in his days as a Member of Parliament. So I suggest it might be more productive to take a rather different tack.'

Suddenly there was a crashing in the thick undergrowth at the edge of the clearing and a brace of wild goats emerged pursued by half a dozen of the bewigged children carrying automatic rifles. The chase plunged back into the jungle of thorn bushes and there was a sustained burst of gunfire.

'I have a dream,' said Taylor, turning to Lady Ethne and beaming, 'but it's of goat casserole again I fear.'

Another salvo.

'Or goat mince,' chuckled Lady Jardine laying a hand lightly on Charles Taylor's arm. 'But the cost of entertaining being prohibitive these days let's try to reduce the number of your dinner guests by at least six.'

A couple of hours later her overloaded car rolled up to the Liberian frontier. Colin Shwartz and his men, wearing nothing but their identity discs, unwound themselves from the sweaty ruck in the back seat. Mrs Armitage and Mrs Butler were dusted down and chattered about their jolly exciting morning, all the while taking in the finer points of the scene of embarrassed Olympian athleticism around them. Ethne Jardine was having a conversation with Ambassador Reeves on the tank radio.

'In return I've apologised...'

'Apaalagized...'

'For your flagrant breach of the rules and agreed to a couple of minor concessions....'

'Caansessions...'

'Perhaps it's escaped your attention, Ambassador, but concessions are the common currency of professional negotiation unlike your unfortunate penchant for naked aggression.' At the mention of 'naked' she gave an appreciative glance in Shwartz' direction.

'This is quite imprapper...'

'But impressive you have to concede – the result I mean ...and no doubt you can discuss the finer points of propriety with Sir Henry at the next Joint Powers but in the meantime your peace keepers are safely on their way home and in return I've agreed that we'll review the Liberian aid programme – no promises, just a review – and that President Taylor will be allowed his long requested State Visit to the Central African Republic as soon as the details can be thrashed out. Now will you be so kind as to instruct your tank commander to turn his machine round, or whatever he does, and give your peacekeepers a lift over the border before they get a serious case of sunburn.'

Reeves spluttered, but finding himself completely out of naked aggression eventually bawled through the static 'WITHDRAAA'.

***

John Prescott belched as he looked down The Mall towards Buckingham Palace from his Grace and Favour flat above Admiralty arch. He was suffering from a mixture of dyspepsia (after a black pudding breakfast so monstrous the World Health Organisation were probably preparing a warning leaflet about it as he belched) and a nagging depression (which occasionally surfaced if he allowed himself to dwell on the fact that his Socialist torch had long since been doused in the wells of patronage). Dressed, if so it could be described, in a string vest and saggy Y fronts which would have had him banned from any self respecting Armani outlet, he still looked like a card carrying member of the mob at the Palace gates but he feared his rabble rousing days were over. He often stood here nurturing the faint hope that, at the other end of the Mall, Phil the Greek had his binoculars out and was being reminded that the British working classes hadn't all gone away to Torremolinos.

The entry phone link from back door security squawked to say his visitor had arrived and he dragged himself away from his imagined Prince-baiting and threw on a silk dressing gown that wouldn't have been out of place adorning a minor royal. By the time the door bell rang he'd settled into his other role as the blunt but affable Deputy P.M.

'Harry Tinsley as I live and breathe. How long's it been? Twenty years, twenty five?'

'About. We've all worn a bit, right enough. But it's a comfort you're every bit as fat as you look on the box.'

'Aye it's the worry that puts the weight on, Harry. You just don't know the burdens us servants of the people have to bear. Affairs of State and all that bollocks.'

'You wouldn't recognise worry if it jumped up and grabbed you by the crown jewels. Unless you've changed a bit. Mebbe you're having one of them mid life crisis things. I hear there's a lot of them going off down here. Mebbe that dressing gown's a symptom.'

Harry Tinsley was a tall, muscular man, slightly stooped and with big hands beaten into frying pans by the years he spent on trawlers in Icelandic waters. But then he made a fortunate landfall, married a rich skipper's widow and bought shares in the first of his fleet of freighters and tankers.

'Anyhow, I don't suppose you've asked me down to give you a medical so what's it all about?'

'I just wanted to consult an old friend who knows more about sommat as I do.'

'Bugger me you must be ill if you're owning up to not knowing sommat. Don't often hear one of you lot doing that.'

'Golden rule, Harry. Never own up in public less you're after the sympathy vote. Or in private when a civil servant's listening because they've had their sympathy surgically removed. In here it's probably all right though. I haven't found any bugs back to Campbell's bunker yet.'

'So?'

'So I hear you're doing a bit of supply work for the Foreign Office and the M.O.D.'

'So?'

'So I'm interested in finding one or two things out about the

Joint Powers Western African Federation.'

'Ah. No can do. We're trussed up in the Official Secrets Act tighter than Hazel Lewthwaite's knicker elastic.'

At school Prescott had spent some months with an itch for the pneumatic Miss Lewthwaite. 'Harry Tinsley. I never knew you went out with Hazel.'

'Only a couple of trips round the back of the bike sheds when she was pissed off with you for one reason or another.'

'You sly old sod. She never told me.'

'Maybe she didn't want to embarrass you with comparisons. Anyhow why are you asking me about African Federations when you could just stroll into the Foreign Office and pull rank?'

'Well now, that's an official secret too, but just let's say that it's a bit like you and Hazel Lewthwaite. I'd rather none of the buggers knew I was sniffing about.'

'I still don't understand why you've got an interest in foreign parts all of a sudden. In Hull you used to think Grimsby was foreign.'

'Still do, Harry, still do. Only explanation I can think of why their eyes are so close together. I once worked with some Grimsby lads on the ferries. They could as easy have come from Afghanisoddingstan for all the sense you could get out of them.'

'Isn't being racist and Grimsbyist in the same sentence a bit politically incorrect for shiny New Labour?'

'Everybody knows I don't understand sentences, Harry, but bottom line I don't like being pissed about and I particularly don't like being pissed about by snotty creeps like our Foreign friggin' Secretary so just between you and me I think him and Blair are keeping me in the dark and it's something to do with this Western African Federation job which is why I'm keeping you from your aperitifs at Claridges and forgiving you for shagging Hazel Lewthwaite when my back was turned or more likely when her back was turned and is that a long enough sentence for you?'

'Not as long as the one I'd be facing if it got out I'd been talking about our shipping runs to the Federation.'

'But it won't get out Harry. We never met and you didn't tell me anything. If I ever do have to explain how I got to know... certain things... I'll blame it on the mole in the Ministry. Everybody else does.' Prescott stood up and held open the dressing gown. 'See no hidden microphones, no two way mirrors just an old school mate who needs a little favour.'

'And an underwear consultant. If you were wearing that sort of kit when you were sixteen it's no wonder Hazel Lewthwaite played away.' He scribbled a note on a scrap of paper. 'But in the meantime, having seen that vision of northern manliness in all its horrible glory I'm going to take pity on you and give you two bits of advice myself. First, don't take up modelling and, second, if you're looking to find out about the Western African Federation don't start in Western Africa.'

CHAPTER THREE

Dee Reeves, the American ambassador's wife was, by common consent, common. She'd travelled effortlessly from pulchritudinous cheerleader to blousey early middle age without ever managing to improve her taste or take the edge off her dimness, according to the lady members of the Jamestown English club at any rate.

But in her company Pike found himself in the eye of a storm of incipient lust and imagined misdemeanour. Tonight the storm was raging particularly fiercely round the Reeves' flat. Pike had been invited up for a private word. When the summons came it had all been a bit cloak and dagger. She wanted to ask him a big, juicy favour and nobody had to know about it. So it was he found himself perched on the edge of a sofa with Mrs Reeves pouring the drinks at a vast corner cocktail cabinet that would have been more at home in a casino on the Las Vegas Strip than in the private quarters of the American Ambassador.

A throaty giggle. 'Don't look so nervous Mr. Pike. I aint gonna eat you.'

Shame, thought Pike.

And she was most certainly dressed for dinner. Shrink wrapped in a short but lurid carmine number that, from where Pike was sitting, seemed to plunge from here to eternity.

'Oh no, not nervous. Just tired after a stressful Ship Day.'

She sat down close beside him on the sofa and having arranged the plunging 'here' to best effect slowly crossed her long legs apparently blocking the path to eternity. 'Now this little favour Mr. Pike...'

Pike was having difficulty hearing her because of the thunder and lightning crashing about in his head.

'Are you O.K., You've gone a little pale.'

'No, I'm just fine, Mrs. Reeves. Cheers. And so what can I do for you?'

'Well it's no great big thing really but I just know that Donald would make such a fuss about it if I told him and he's so busy and I really don't want to bother him.'

'Ye-es?'

She shifted position and brushed against Pike's arm. 'I really want to go swimming.'

'Swimming.' Pike had already picked the bikini. 'But you've got a swimming pool in the basement, Mrs. Reeves.'

'No. Proper swimming.' Off came the imagined bikini. 'In Prosperous Bay.

For a brief moment common sense overcame adolescence. 'Oh I don't think that would be wise, Mrs. Reeves. They're big seas up there and anyhow it's a long way off, far side of the Central African Republic.'

'Yes, Donald thought it was too difficult when I mentioned it to him, but he's just a silly old thing when it comes to…adventures.'

Pike was already swinging from liana to liana to rescue his heroine from death by boredom.

'And you know as well as I do, Richard, that we could whizz up there for a day and nobody would ever know. Cept us.'

'Us?' The tropical storm in Pike's head gave way to the Aurora Borealis.

'Well I couldn't go scootin' off on my own, silly. That *would* be reckless. But with your experience, and if we picked a day when Donald was busy with Joint Staffs or something. Easy.'

Pike's afternoon had drifted into slow motion with a glistening surf rolling lazily through the Ambassador's living room and a tanned and naked Mrs Reeves a mermaid in the swell. 'There's a Joint Staffs meeting on Tuesday.' He said in rather a rush.

'I just knew you'd think of a way.' Said Mrs Reeves jumping up, clapping her hands and leaning forward to kiss him lightly on the forehead.

'Yes it's an Extraordinary that Ambassador Reeves asked for earlier this afternoon,' whispered Pike looking deep into another softly rising swell.

The cares of Ship Day had slipped their moorings and begun to sail away until Pike remembered that before he got even a glimpse of bikini he'd have to square the protocols with Bokassa.

***

'He wants to play the bloody bagpipes.'

Henry Jardine was slumped in a chair drowning the memory of his trip to Kampala.

'As if murdering half the bloody country and throwing people tag lag to the crocodiles weren't bad enough, now he wants to torture the ones that are left with the bloody bagpipes.'

'We'll just have to get the ODA to fund a sound-proofed rehearsal room,' said Lady Jardine, forever practical.

Sir Henry groaned at the thought of submitting yet another bizarre request to the incredulous civil servants of the Overseas Development Administration. 'And of course he's demanding we order them from the Queens Bagpipe Maker and he wants Her Majesty to pick up the bill and he insists the said bagpipe maker should henceforth be By Appointment to the King of Scotland.'

'Oh, dear.'

'Precisely. Well Pike can negotiate with Lord Lyon King of Arms because this'll test his bloody heraldic skills to destruction. Madman rampant on a field gules strangling the natives with one hand and Kenneth McKellar with the other. It should just look a bloody picture above the door of a croft on Loch Lomond, or wherever the Queen has her bagpipes made.'

Sir Henry sank deeper into his diplomatic gloom and Lady Jardine replenished his drink.

'I've had quite a busy day, too, dear.' She ran through the details of the tank invasion of Liberia and that awful buffoon Donald Reeves and the rescue of the peacekeepers ('Not a stitch on my dear') and the negotiations with Charles Taylor and that the Americans were incandescent and demanding an emergency Joint Staffs. By the time she'd finished, the haunting image of a bloodstained Idi Amin leading the massed bands of the Highland Division down the Esplanade in the Edinburgh Military Tattoo had all but faded.

Sir Henry shook himself from one nightmare into another. *'He sent the bloody tank into Liberia?'*

'I'm afraid he did, dear. But fortunately Mrs Butler and Mrs Armitage were a match for him.'

'I don't wish to appear ungrateful, Ethne, but we really shouldn't have to rely on the bloody W.I. to keep the Americans in check. We're not the United Nations.'

At which point the London telephone rang.

'Foreign Secretary….' Sir Henry grimaced and Lady Ethne lay back on the sofa and mimed tickling her stomach. Henry spluttered. 'No, Foreign Secretary, just a peeled grape going down the wrong way.' The telephone jabbered and Henry held it at arm's length. When the handset subsided the Ambassador put it back to his ear. 'Problem, yes. But we've sorted it out. The indians are lying drunk in a corner and we've managed to get the cowboys back into the fort.' Sir Henry's attempt at humour apparently didn't play well in the distant, lofty halls of the Foreign and Commonwealth office. 'No, Foreign Secretary, I didn't know about the leak. Of course I'm aware of how delicate a situation....' The London line sounded like a hive of angry bees for some minutes, long enough for Sir Henry to replenish his scotch. '....Yes, Foreign Secretary, but the reports you've had appear to be wrong in one crucial respect if I may be so bold. It was the Americans that caused the bloody problem rather than, as they seem to claim, solving it. And if I may be blunt, Foreign Secretary, I'd find it so much easier to keep the pot off the boil, so to speak, if our trusted allies didn't attempt to re-stage the bloody D Day landings every time my back's turned.' A couple of minutes of what seemed to Lady Ethne to be rather more emollient jabbering brought the call to an end.

'Well, well. There's a turn up. It seems we have the great man's approval to give Reeves a rogering,' said Sir Henry as he replaced the old, red bakelite hand set. 'Not because our esteemed boss is giving wholehearted support to his beleaguered troops in distant parts you understand, but because there's a shipment coming in later in the month on the container run that they're trying to slide past the Americans. And they think if Reeves is still stamping his foot about the Liberia business he's less likely to notice.'

'So the F.O.'s taken up armed amateur dramatics again.' Ethne sighed as she tidied an unruly wisp of hair by the mirror.

'And that's a recipe for buggering up the casserole. As history forefends,' said Henry gloomily. But they still went in to dinner relishing the thought of roasted American Ambassador tomorrow.

***

In the Villa Kolongo the stifling heat of the afternoon lay like a shroud across the trappings of Empire. It had settled on the worm eaten woodwork and peeling gilt of the Imperial throne, on the mangy cat sleeping on one of the throne's outstretched eagle wings, on the rusting suit of mediaeval armour propped incongruously under a garden centre umbrella in a gloomy corner and on the stooped and dark suited Chef de Cabinet who was shuffling, almost imperceptibly across bare boards towards the Thirteenth Apostle.

'Highness.' The word came like a hint of a breeze but there was no response.

'Highness.' A little louder. A rheumy eye opened. 'Monsieur Pike requests an audience.'

The man slumped in an overstuffed armchair wheezed awake. As he moved springs jangled deep within the threadbare upholstery. A spasm of the man's left hand swept an array of pill boxes and potion jars from a small table onto the floor. With his other hand he snapped up an ivory topped cane as if fending off the latest assassination attempt.

'Why Pike?' A trembling voice.

'Because he's here, Highness.'

'Why not Jardine?'

'Because he isn't.'

'Once it would have been Queen herself. And now, le valet.' He struggled to sit upright.

'Dignité. Unite. Travail.' A croaked echo of a once Imperial motto. The old man's chin sank back onto his chest.

Unwilling or unable to turn, the Chef de Cabinet frantically beckoned an arm behind his back and Pike had to duck as stepped into the room. The sounds of Bangui town drifted in through the open window as he waited for the untidy heap of white clothes in the chair to speak again. Emperor Jean-Bedel Bokassa, Marshall of Africa, Grand Master of the International Brotherhood of Knights Collectors of Postage Stamps eventually stirred.

'Monsieur Pike you find me unwell.' A voice like a run down clock.

'I'm sorry to hear that, Highness. May we invite the British medical centre staff to attend?'

'My doctor is here.' He reached out a scrawny hand and grasped the tall metal crucifix that stood to one side of his chair. The figure of a black Christ streaked with blood rocked slightly as the yellowing talons withdrew into the bundle of clothes. Pike wondered when Christ had found time to write the prescriptions for the well stocked pharmacy that seemed to occupy most available surfaces in the room. Pike glanced towards the servant who scowled and nodded at the same time. 'Ambassador Jardine sends his compliments and requests passage for certain accredited representatives of Her Majesty's Overseas Development Administration – myself and my assistant actually – as part of the ongoing Joint Staffs coastal survey......'

The Emperor's dark-ringed eyes clicked open. 'Espionage.'

'Oh, no, most certainly not, Highness' said Pike, rather offended by the suggestion. 'Merely routine administration. Tying up loose ends.'

'We have no loose ends here, Mr Pike. Loose ends were abolished by La Decree Imperiale. As we all know loose ends can be woven into all manner of evils in dark corners.'

From a dark corner of Pike's memory rose the spectre of how Bokassa had once tied up the loose ends of an attempted student rebellion. The bodies of the leaders were found trussed up in the freezers in the basement of one of his palaces.

'It was an unfortunate phrase, Highness. Bureaucracy. Nothing more. But there's so much of it about these days. Can't spend fourpence halfpenny without writing a hundred page report. What I should have said is that we're sorting out the detail of a World Bank grant application for investment in coastal defences.' Pike had learned over the years that the words 'bank' and 'grant' usually managed to defuse the most difficult of situations.

'L'addition sil vous plait.'

'Approximately 23 million US if I can sign off the paperwork.'

'And paid where?'

'Through the usual channels, Highness. France or Switzerland and, as ever, into the account you nominate.'

Pike knew he could slide a mere twenty three million through The Fund with very little difficulty. It was one of the great successes of the Administration. Money was paid to Heads of State into marked accounts that were effectively locked except for the odd bit of petty cash. After a decent interval they were officially frozen on some pretext or other at which point the money was transferred back into the kitty. It was a delightfully simple, stately gavotte. The money kept doing the rounds, oiling the diplomacy. In capitals like Bangui, the countries where the accounts supposedly lay such as France or Switzerland or The Cayman Islands were accused of treachery. The crooks didn't really know how much money they had stashed away anyhow and the Joint Staffs finance officers came up smelling of nothing.

'Vous avez la permission, Monsieur Pike. There will of course be un charge minimale for the necessary paperwork.' Bokassa seemed to have brightened. The bowed Chef de Cabinet conjured a sheaf of papers heavy with wax seals from his jacket. Sweeping away several jars of liniment he made space for them on a table thick with drifts of dust and offered Pike a gold fountain pen.

He signed and appended the diplomatic seal and made his escape. After he'd gone the servant turned slowly to Bokassa and sniggered like a snuffling animal. 'And we don't even have a coast.'

***

'Aanforgiveable.... Aanacceptable.... Aanprofessional.' Reeves' roars of protest were echoing to the rafters of the Castle Hall. The secretariat staff shuffled and occasionally coughed and seemed to be taking a greater than normal interest in the briefing papers piled on the long oak table. Only Sir Henry, in an ornately carved chair at the head of the table and partly silhouetted against the high, heraldic window that looked out onto Jamestown Square, was perfectly still. Reeves' apoplexy lurched from the security of the Colony to the intrusions of non-diplomatic staff to Liberian disloyalty. Clauses and sub clauses of Atlantic Rules were thrashed around the room until Reeves reached his crescendo.

'The President of the United States has been informed. Personally.'

He remained standing to watch the full impact of his statement grip the assembled company.

'Jolly good,' said Sir Henry after a decent pause. 'And when do you anticipate we'll hear the President's reasoned response Mr. Ambassador?' The word 'reasoned' spoken with just the tiniest hint of disbelief.

'In due course and after the usual caansultations in Waashington and the Pentagon,' said Reeves, slightly deflated by the fact that the shufflings and the coughings were carrying on pretty much as before. 'But in the interim...'

'In the meantime, Mr. Reeves, all Joint Staffs committees and initiatives will be suspended as outlined in 347 sub clause 4 and as the United States is the initiator of the proceedings, under the terms of 782 sub paragraph 16, Her Majesty's Government in consultation with the United Nations will assume Colony control until the matter is satisfactorily resolved. Splendid. Meeting adjourned.'

Sir Henry banged the oak gavel which set the dust dancing in a shaft of light sparkling red and gold through the stained glass. He rose and started for the door. The clerks hurriedly scooped up armfuls of paper from the table. Reeves subsided. Sir Henry turned as he was leaving the room and beamed more brightly than the window. 'Oh, by the way Donald, Ethne sends her *very* best wishes.'

***

What Pike was wishing at that precise moment couldn't be spoken. Beside him in the rattling Morris Ambassador Dee Reeves fidgeted and chattered loudly about nothing in particular as they headed for the sea. Clouds of choking dust rose behind the car as it crested the final rise and the route they'd taken across the low hills was marked out by a line of hazy red that hung in the still air. Ahead, Prosperous Plain was suddenly spread out below them. Rollers tumbled in from the Atlantic and crashed at the foot of the headlands enclosing the bay.

'Perfect, Mr. Pike, just perfect,' she shrieked and clapped her hands.

Pike thought that within the hour he'd be the judge of that. As the car turned down the switchback road to the beach, Mrs Reeves grabbed her bag from the back seat and began a contortion of changing only partially concealed by a strategically placed but rather small Stars and Stripes towel.

'I think it would be a good idea if you kept your eyes on the road, Mr. Pike.' Said with a twinkle in her voice. The car lurched over a rock which dislodged the towel and Pike wrenched the wheel to take the next left hander which he could just see past an undulating landscape that he recognised from his dreams. The car slithered to a halt, Mrs. Reeves jumped out and, having lost her chosen bikini somewhere in the footwell, shrugged and smiled before turning away and running naked to the sea. Pike thought he might have a problem getting into his trunks.

But twenty minutes later, after a waddle across the beach, the cold waters of the Atlantic had solved the problem. Mrs. Reeves was a powerful swimmer and struck out for the far headland with Pike trailing along in her wake. Every so often she'd stop and bob up among the rollers. Being provocative or just checking that her chaperone was still breathing. Unfortunately the open mouthed anticipation caused by momentary glimpses of a glistening Dee Reeves rising through the surf were causing the floundering Pike to swallow more Atlantic than was good for him. By the time he reached the flat rocks where the mermaid of his imagination had pulled herself out of the water he was spluttering like a motorboat about to run out of fuel. She reached down and hauled him ashore. He lay gasping on the rock until a shadow fell across his face. When he dared to open his eyes two years and forty seven days of anticipation came to life. She kissed him lightly on the forehead and said 'Mr Pike you've just made my day.'

A siren went off in Pike's head. As Mrs. Reeves sat up the siren blew again and out of the corner of his eye Pike saw the bulky stern of a container ship edging out from behind the headland. Mrs Reeves waved and there was an appreciative cheer and round of applause from the crew lining the rail. Pike tried to hide behind her; tried to pretend he wasn't there but that was made considerably more difficult by Mrs. Reeves standing up, holding her arms wide and turning slowly to show off her glistening body to the very best effect before diving into the sea.

As the ship manoeuvred and began to disappear again the crew strained to catch a final glimpse of the swimmer who lazily rolled onto her back and waved again. Pike, meanwhile, made himself scarce behind the rocks and, keeping his head down, worked his way to the nose of the headland to a point where he could look round into the next bay. What he saw was very curious, as much of an apparition to him as Dee Reeves had been to the ship's crew. A fully equipped harbour, deserted apart from the berthing Tinsley Line ship, in a place where no harbour officially existed.

As he headed back to the car Pike saw that she'd got there before him.

'You look hot and bothered, Mr. Pike.' She was drying herself off with the little stars and stripes.

He started to tell her that he was actually bothered about the harbour and the ship docking in the next cove but thought better of it. But then she asked him to be a good boy and dry the bits she couldn't reach and suddenly he didn't care if the entire Russian Navy was just around the corner. The sirens started to go off in his head again but this time there were no ships in sight.

CHAPTER FOUR

The President of the Royal Geographical Society had been amazed when he was told the Deputy Prime Minister would make time to open their new exhibition celebrating the Giants of African Exploration. Normally he'd have been palmed off with, at best, an unknown but pompous back bencher from Mexborough or some such benighted place. When John Prescott actually found his way to the Society's headquarters in Kensington Gore Lord Chorlton was doubly amazed.

He'd been a bit concerned about making conversation with a man who, on television at least, seemed to have raised gobbledegook to an art form. But Prescott in the flesh turned out to be a surprisingly jolly cove.

'Lord Chorlton I presume...' hand outstretched as he stepped through the creaking doors into a musty Victorian hallway. 'But where's the pith helmet?'

'Oh, they went out with native bearers and Conservative government, Deputy Prime Minister. Not cool.... except of course they were.'

'Wouldn't know. Never wore one. You'd get funny looks in a pith helmet in some bits of Hull. And the only native bearers we have are in the strip club in Quay Street. Anyoff, lead on to the heart of darkness your lordship.'

It was an odd speech with its references to Humphrey Bogart and the African Queen, Shangri La and King Solomon's Mines. No mention was made of any of the real explorers but the tape was eventually cut, the exhibition opened and the embarrassment limited. After the press rabble had been encouraged to leave and the sparkling white replaced by champagne the board and trustees were treated to a Prescott critique of the evils of empire. The great explorers were at best pederasts and at worst missionaries. The British stood on the necks of the blacks in the same way coal owners trampled the miners and Thatcherites stuffed the unemployed. Obviously it was all down to public school education – homosexuality, fagging (and I know that's nowt to do with woodbines before you say) and inadequate nappy training. But not necessarily in that order.

'Obvious when you think about it.'

Lord Chorlton, who was having difficulty with the obvious, listened politely. Eventually he was bold enough to note that quite a number of former colonies had descended into what looked remarkably like chaos since independence.

'You've been at the Daily Mail again. Educated chap like you shouldn't believe everything you read in the toilet papers.' He held out his champagne glass for a refill and warmed to his theme. 'Take the African Federation. Odd spot of bother now and then, but now we've got the development plans working and done deals with Amin and Bokassa and the rest of them everything's hunky dory.'

'But what's this we've been reading about Liberia?' Asked Lord Chorlton, determined to stir the cannibals' pot.

'Neither nowt nor summat. You take it from me as knows, Taylor's signed up. Lot of brass going in through the Joint Powers. Five year plans, defence treaties the bloody lot.'

The great and the good of the Royal Geographical society nodded in disagreement rather in the way of model dogs in the rear window of a Ford Anglia. Prescott, meanwhile, ratched in his pockets for the bit of paper he'd been given by Harry Tinsley which was the real reason for him wasting valuable time in a nest of imperial apologists.

'Anyoff, enough of this setting the world to rights malarkey. I need to do a spot of research on what looks to me like sommat to do with maps and I thought the Royal Geographical Society would be a better bet than Marks and Spencers.'

He handed the paper to Lord Chorlton. It read; 1595S570W

'So whereabouts in Africa's that?' Then with a broad smile.

'Question in the Members bar general knowledge quiz. Hadn't a clue.'

Resisting the temptation to wholeheartedly agree, Lord Chorlton led the way to the ornate Mercator globe by the leaded window and let his finger run over lines of longitude and latitude.

'It must have been a trick question, Deputy Prime Minister, because this map reference is all of twelve hundred miles from Africa.'

His finger pointed to a solitary dot in an expanse of blue grey. As Prescott bent down to bring the antique lettering into focus he saw the name - St. Helena.

'Most remote island in the world. They used to call it the Atlantic Alcatraz.'

'Well bugger me,' said Prescott. 'I think I just won.'

***

Terry Hanrahan was losing his battle with the Atlantic. The rumble of an angry ocean roared along the hull as he bounced off the walls of the cramped lower decks cabin where he'd spent many hours nursing a sick bucket for the past twelve days. And still another two to go. He clattered against the edge of the bunk from which a nasty lurch of the ship had extracted him onto the floor a few seconds before.

The mail boat RMS St. Helena was ploughing its way through the longest delivery round in the world. From Cardiff to Capetown via Ascension Island in mid Atlantic. Then 800 miles to the south east to St. Helena and, once a year, another 1200 miles to the south west to Tristan da Cunha. If he hadn't been trying to reach the bucket again Hanrahan might have been counting his blessings that he was only going as far as St. Helena to take up his new job with the island's Cable and Wireless radio relay station. Instead, as a particularly vicious wave lifted and shook the ship, he remembered that when he'd first seen the advertisement for the job he'd thought it was in St. Helens. The image of a sun-drenched and stable Lancashire industrial town taunted him.

'Damned funny people the Saints by the sound of it.' The sound being that of Bloor in the top bunk who was trying to keep focus on his constantly moving guide book to St. Helena. 'Half African, quarter Chinese with a dash of Malaya, Madagascar, Malibar and a soupcon of European thrown in. They must be brownish yellowish grey.'

'I don't think it works like that.' Hanrahan retched.

'I wouldn't be too sure. You look a rather similar colour dear boy.' Glancing over his half spectacles. 'And according to this the Island's overrun with bastards....'

'So's this cabin.'

'No, proper bastards.'

'Like I said, so's this cabin.'

'I mean Illyjollygitimates dear chap. They call 'em 'spares'. Obviously not the place to be an underprivileged piccaninny.'

'Can't offhand think of anywhere that is,' said Hanrahan.

'And their staple food is yams because apparently that's the only thing the millions of rats infesting the place don't make off with.'

'Are you thinking of leaving this sinking ship then?'

'Not at this precise moment. But at least there aren't any snakes on St. Helena.'

'Maybe Saint Patrick's been here before us in his bloody coracle.'

Hanrahan and Bloor were, like most double acts, chalk and cheese. Terry Hanrahan tall and slim if, temporarily, a rather strange colour; Theo Bloor on the ruddy and raddled side of bohemian. Hanrahan the trusty technician; Bloor the artist and writer, or so it said in his passport.

'Says there are a helluvalot of sharks though. Just as well I have a natural antipathy to water.'

'Speaking from personal experience I've never been much bothered by sharks in the shower.' To Hanrahan's certain knowledge Bloor hadn't troubled the soap dish since Cardiff.

'Ah, but ever since I made the mistake of seeing Jaws I've

41

always kept my legs crossed in the heads...' The picture that rose on the swells of ocean and nausea was too horrible for Hanrahan to contemplate.

Bloor swung his legs onto the floor, straightened his waistcoat of many colours and snuff stains and announced himself to be ready for a hearty breakfast. 'I've been telling you since Ascension, dear boy, that what you need is a slaver of greasy fried bread and sweet tea with condensed milk. Guaranteed cure.' As the cabin door swung shut with a clatter Hanrahan retched again into the bucket.

Bloor looked across the almost empty passengers' dining room. As usual at this time of the morning only the military were on parade. To the accompaniment of cruets and coffee pots tinkling in time with the changing notes of the ship's engines he set a course through the shoals of tables to where Brigadier Birtwistle was holding court on the far side of the room.

'Theo, come and join us.' Alec Birtwistle was on manoeuvres through a heaped breakfast plate.

'Morning, brigadier. I was just thinking it has to be a sign of advancing years when even the top brass are getting to look younger. Surely it's against Queen's Regs. to be a brigadier without side whiskers and gout.' The junior officers took their cue from Birtwistle and part rose from their seats as Bloor sat down. Some of them were of a greenish hue but none of them would have dared miss the brigadier's invitation to breakfast.

'And presumably because you're an artistic chappie you're a deranged, alcoholic shirt lifter.' Another salient of sausages disappeared and a ripple of rather nervous laughter came from the juniors' end of the table.

'Only when the spirit takes me, dear chap.'

As the waiter took Bloor's order of porridge, kippers and a large Chivas Regal, Bloor noticed that the Saint on breakfast duties was a fairly normal browny-beige. A grey-green Captain who, to Theodore Bloor, looked to be all of fourteen years old turned the conversation to Brigadier Birtwistle's new posting.

'Bit different from the foot and mouth campaign, sir.' The

Brigadier had made a name for himself in the mass grave business, sorting out the Government's bungled attempts to contain the disease, burying sheep and cattle in Northern England and threatening to bury any bovine politician who strayed into his field.

'So what are you going to be doing on Saint Helena?' Theo asked as he ladled cream onto his porridge.

'Oh, can't tell you that, Theo. Toppest of top secrets. Which probably means that they who must be obeyed in London haven't decided yet. Either that or the Min. of Ag. has persuaded Blair to have me sent into exile.' In case exile also entailed starvation Birtwistle swept the last of the fried bread into his mouth leaving the plate so clean that the gilt crest of the RMS St. Helena sparkled. "Anyhow what brings a distinguished artiste on the voyage to hell?'

'Oh, no secrets about my trip. British Council. They pay and their cheques rarely bounce.'

'And what are they getting for their money?'

'Perception. Sensitivity. More precisely a study in words and pictures of the cultural complexity of a melting pot of humanity cut off like Darwin's finches from the rest of civilisation. All to be encapsulated in an art work and an exhibition which will throw light into dark corners of a troubled world.'

'So we'll likely get it in Aldershot then.'

But Birtwistle had had enough culture for one morning and changed the subject.

'Where are you going to be staying?'

'One of the perks of British Council work – British Embassy. It'll probably have all the dubious charm of a crumbling seaside hotel at Lytham St. Anne's and a cast of characters out of Thomas Hardy but at least there'll be a supply of half decent scotch and a toilet that's rather more than a hole in the floor.'

'Don't dare complain, Theo, I think you've got the better deal. Afraid it's Jack Daniels, motherhood and apple pie for us. We've been billeted with the Americans and I think Jude the Obscure is marginally preferable to Arnie Swarzenegger. But duty calls. Hands across the sea and all that.' At which point the sea apparently

43

objected to its name being taken in vain. The ship plunged into a deep trough and half a dinner service made a bid for freedom shattering spectacularly as the waiter did his impression of a fourth division goalkeeper on a bad day.

***

'I'm telling you the bloody ship doesn't exist.'

'But Sir Henry I saw it and, more important, I saw the harbour.'

'Take my word for it, Pike, the harbour doesn't exist either. And that's official. And final.'

'If it's as final as all that, why have we officially built a harbour that doesn't exist and why are officially fictitious shiploads of non-existent containers being landed there?' Pike was getting more exasperated by the minute.

'Well if we're going to be bloody existentialist.....'

'Don't tell me. *You* don't exist either.'

'Of course I bloody exist otherwise you'd be in charge and just imagine what a bloody mess we'd be in then.'

'Maybe *I* don't exist which would solve your imagined problem.'

'He's been sniffing the sherry again...' When Sir Henry switched to abuse in the third person a blown fuse was imminent. Pike backed off.

'Perhaps we should start again at the beginning, Sir. Just to help a simple soul like me to understand a complicated, if non-existent, issue.'

'Right.' Sir Henry spoke as if talking to someone only recently acquainted with English. 'Mr. Pike, you may or may not have seen (or imagined) certain things which, if they existed (but we've established they probably don't)... if they existed they could be of considerable embarrassment to Her Majesty's administration. Fortunately in their non-existence that embarrassment is, if not prevented, at least made less likely?' Pike looked as unconvinced by the finer points of Sir Henry's argument as would the average Bosnian refugee.

44

The Ambassador swept past the sherry to the Glen Morangie and the conversation was held in suspended animation until the glass of amber inspiration had been drained once and refilled.

'...Yes, less likely. Having said that, certain plans are being considered. (And as we know a gulf of administrative incompetence runs between consideration and full blown implementation.) Certain plans are being considered, the existence of which it would be inconvenient for us to acknowledge at this moment. If, however, the presently unacknowledged child of the union between bollocks and aspiration should be delivered we will have known it since its inception. Is that clear?'

Pike felt more comfortable. He realised that for Sir Henry to embark on an explanation that ran so close to the shoals of political correctness meant they were both out of their depth.

'You mean they didn't tell you about it either?'

A long draught from the whisky glass. 'Put it this way, Richard....'

First names were another bad omen.

'...I've been aware of the theoretical pregnancy for some time but your seemingly impossible yet surprisingly detailed observations mean the confinement could be closer than I'd imagined.'

A brooding silence.

'Put another way the conniving bastards are trying to shaft us again. But the one good thing is that we know more about what head office is up to now than we did an hour ago. And the real bonus is that it's only you who saw it.'

Pike blushed but Sir Henry didn't notice having gone back to the glen of tranquillity.

***

The robing had almost been too much for Bokassa but duty demanded it. Even with the help of the wooden frame behind his back, which held the heavy scarlet train trimmed in faux ermine, he wilted. All he was supporting was the Imperial crown, a thin agglomeration of brass gilt and nylon velvet. Even so the weight of it was making him nod uncontrollably. His was a wizened head existing somewhere between prehistory and Parkinson's disease. But duty to his people demanded that he remain, literally, at his post until the formalities were over.

He heard the car arrive. He heard his Chef de Cabinet welcome his guest by the road. He heard voices slowly approaching through a haze of pain and incontinence. He heard the door creak open but he daren't turn his head for fear he would lose his precarious balance.

'His Excellency the Preseedent of Laaberia,' wheezed rather than declaimed and followed by a snigger subsumed in a cough.

Bokassa leaned harder on the crown-topped staff and Charles Taylor with the heavily armed Tasawe at his shoulder stepped into the Emperor's line of vision.

'Brother in power and glory.'

'Yo, bruttha,' said Tasawe through a ganja haze.

Taylor's sharp look bounced off his glazed eyes.

'Brother in divine succession, we bring fraternal greetings. Health and happiness to your Imperial Majesty, prosperity forever in your blessed land." As he said it Taylor saw that he was probably already too late on all counts.

'Welcome to Bangui, mon ami, and may the sun of righteousness forever shine on the face of your nation, aussi.' Barely audible. Taylor had to lean closer to hear the slow, croaking whisper of the man once feared as Papa Bok. Bokassa summoned the strength to bang the staff three times on the dusty boards to end the formal welcome. A rat ran out from under the scarlet velvet and scurried into a corner. Painfully slow, Bokassa shuffled forwards in what had once been pearl encrusted slippers. He left the cloak and train hanging like an abandoned fancy dress costume on the frame as he emerged like a wrinkled insect from a chrysalis. Taylor took his arm and eased him onto a frayed chaise longue. Even the old man's featherweight made the springs tinkle and there was a rustling under the upholstery which suggested that residents in its dark recesses had been disturbed. The Chef de Cabinet divested Bokassa of the crown which was leaning at a precarious angle following the Emperor's efforts to sit down. Stuffing it under his arm, he began to serve tea from a dented and verdigrised samovar. A brass plate announced it had been given as a present from the people of Russia to mark the glorious Emperor's coronation.

Insects buzzed in every dusty corner and Tasawe settled down amongst them under the garden umbrella, leaned his gun against the suit of battered armour and promptly went to sleep.

'So what brings you to see us, mon frere?'

'Just to parley about the old days, my friend...'

'Ah, les belle jours...' A wavering smile flickered through the crust of dried food at the corner of Bokassa's mouth.

'And catch up on the news. That's what I told the Joint Staffs I was going to do and as we know it would be a sin to tell a lie.'

The faded Emperor slowly opened one eye. 'News is lies.' He tried to sit forward but spilled his tea. 'No news en Bangui. Nous abolissez la news..' He mimed a claw across the throat. 'Pour encourager les autres."

'But I've got some good news, brother.'

Taylor sipped his tea and waited until the old servant had shuffled out of the room before he went on.

'Amin's back...'

Bokassa's other eye snapped open.

'..and I think it's time the imperial lapdogs bared a fang or two.'

A chuckle disguised as a cough came from behind the closed door.

Whispering close to Bokassa's ear now. 'And we'd be so much more effective if we worked as a pack. Don't you agree, Excellency?'

The pause seemed as long as a Bangui afternoon before the old man laid a claw on Taylor's arm and smiled wistfully. 'You're right, mon frere. I think it's time to restore a little respect.'

Taylor looked at Bokassa and wondered if there was still enough time left.

CHAPTER FIVE

'What's he up to?' mouthed Blair in the Foreign Secretary's direction as Prescott breezed up the corridor to the Prime Minister's office in the House of Commons whistling a robust but strangled version of *If I Ruled The World*.

'And why's our favourite old war horse so spry this morning?' Blair's voice revealing in his cheery greeting that he was as accomplished at sincerity as was Prescott at whistling.

'Oh, just full of the joys. And why not on a morning like this.'

Worrying, thought Blair putting his brave face on.

'I was just thinking when I was having a cuppa with the Kurds down Parliament Square that it's a long time since I've been on a decent picket line.'

'Not recommended in the security manual fraternising with mobs of protesters, John.' By now Blair had his stern face on.

'You know, Tony, if you frown any harder your eyebrows are going to strangle each other.' Prescott laid his hand on Blair's arm and the Prime Minister flinched.

Prescott turned to the Foreign Secretary. 'Never worry, F Sec. They're O.K the Kurds. Right softies I reckon. All they want is a bit of desert they can call Kurdisomethingorother where they can keep their camels. Wouldn't have thought it was much to ask.'

'Unfortunately, John, the 'bit of desert' as you so eloquently describe it happens to be half of Turkey and half of Iraq. And I don't think camels are entirely the issue.'

'Well lah de bloody dah, Kurds and wheyhey. All I was doing was my bit for international goodwill. I thought it's what all us good socialists should be doing. And I got the best cheer of the morning.'

The Foreign Secretary's oleaginous demeanour dripped disapproval. 'Why can't you just stick to by- passes and Council Tax, John, and leave the finer points of international diplomacy to us.'

48

'Why? Do you fancy being the Kurd's best friend then? Or are you still too busy with the African Federation?' The Foreign Secretary started to interject and Prescott beamed. '...Anyoff why are you both looking so piquey? Had a bad canapé at the Palace or has Cherie got you on the colonic aggravation again?' He slapped Tony on the back and marched into the policy committee meeting, playfully nipping Peter Mandelson's bum on the way.

An hour later the bulk of the agenda had been democratically rubber stamped. The usual health and education platitudes had been polished for public display. Unusually, they'd managed to get through the meeting without Tony and Gordon squabbling over the scraps.

Then they got to Foreign Office business.

'Zimbabwe,' said the Foreign Secretary as if summoning a portent. 'We have a particularly delicate situation there. Mugabe seems to be flavour of the month with the African Commonwealth which gives us a negotiating problem when we go to Abuja next week. The Nigerians aren't going to take kindly to what they will inevitably see as the nasty white masters throwing their weight around and bullying poor Robert.'

'Just do the same as we did with Liberia.'

Prescott's unexpected contribution hit the surface of the Cabinet pond and sent a ripple of silence round the table.

'Sorry, John?' The Foreign Secretary looked momentarily disconcerted.

'Liberia. You remember Liberia. Well you would, being Foreign Secretary and all. But just in case it's slipped out of yer briefs I'll give you a clue. Charlie Taylor, rebels, Monrovia surrounded, thousands dead, 'orrible bloody mess.' The Foreign Secretary was now doing a passable impersonation of a coy carp with breathing difficulties. 'Aye, you do remember. I knew you would.'

The Prime Minister rallied to his goldfish's defence.

'Liberia was a totally different situation, John. For one thing the nearest they had to an imperial power was the Americans and, as you'll no doubt recall with your new found interest in foreign affairs, a fine mess they made of sorting out their African back lot.'

'Well the Central African Republic then.'

Like Wimbledon spectators the heads of cabinet members ticked back and forth.

'French. So not in our orbit.'

Advantage Foreign Secretary.

'Uganda?'

The Prescott ace clattered into the woodwork.

'Uganda ...'

His High and Mightiness faded as matchpoint loomed but, urged on by the PM's pitying look, rallied. 'Uganda is an entirely inappropriate comparison.'

Tick tick.

'Don't see why. Amin and Mugabe had one thing in common - apart from being black and barmy. They were both Britain's Mr Nice Guy once.'

Tick.

'Circumstances change. But the real difference is that Amin was kicked out by his own beloved people. Mugabe's keep voting him back in.'

'Hang on. The Ugandans only kicked Amin out after the British slipped a few quid into Tanzania's back pocket to help.'

Jaws around the table dropped as the ministerial heads above them registered that Prescott had actually heard of Tanzania. A number of the owners of those heads hoped that Blair wasn't in schoolmasterly mode; that he wouldn't pick on them to point out where Tanzania was on the map. The Foreign Secretary snapped. 'I don't think swanning off for a week in Bali to discuss international environmental window dressing has entirely prepared you for the complexities of post colonial diplomatic negotiation, John.'

'It taught me a bit about islands though.'

Blank looks around the table except for the almost imperceptible glance from Blair to his Foreign Office Grandee.

'As a point of information, ladies and gentlemen,' said the Prime Minister with a particularly chilly edge to his voice, 'we've decided that maintaining our robust opposition to Mugabe's regime and its abuses of human rights and political process is the only available option. No reversing on this one. Whatever the backsliders in South Africa want us to do. Someone has to hold the line. The wider international community expects no less of us. I take it we're all agreed?'

The chorus of acquiescent mutterings was barely registered by the P.M. as he leaned close to Prescott's left ear. 'Downing Street office in half an hour, John. If the Secretary General of the United Nations can spare you. Which I may not.'

Prescott fluttered the bags under his eyes, smiled broadly and sauntered off to the tea room whistling an unmelodious medley of *Rule Britannia* and *A life on the Ocean wave.*

***

'More tea Mr. Bloor?' Asked Lady Ethne carefully keeping at arms length from her malodorous guest. (She'd already instructed Momo to make sure there was a plastic sheet on his bed and an industrial strength air freshener in the guest bedroom.)

'And for you, Mr Hanrahan? The car will be here shortly to take you up to C and W, but I do believe you're already looking rather better.'

'Well I'm sorry to say your room's still running a heavy sea, Lady Ethne,' said Hanrahan, grimly hanging onto the furniture. 'But no doubt I'll make landfall, or whatever the phrase is, before long.' His tea cup rattled in its saucer as the swell rolled past the bureau.

'And when do the creative juices start to flow, Mr. Bloor?' Asked Sir Henry from behind the obituaries page of one of the batch of Daily Telegraphs that had arrived on the boat.

'Already have, Ambassador,' said Bloor draining his glass. 'But we mustn't rush these things. I'm here for six weeks and I find that gleaning local knowledge has to be an osmotic process.'

'I see Lord Nunburnholme's popped his clogs,' said Sir Henry, whose knowledge of and interest in osmosis was on a par with his knowledge of and fascination with everything elso Bloor was talking about.

51

'Oh dear,' said Lady Jardine, mentally flicking through past dinner party lists.

'Oh dear, nothing. The man was a pratt. Once sold his regimental horse to a bloody hooker. Surprised he was bright enough to die.' He looked accusingly at Bloor over the paper. 'And I see a bloody transvestite potter's won the Turner Prize. Mind you I've always thought modern art was for people who make tits of themselves.' Oblivious to the physiological inexactitude of his remark, he chuckled his way to the whisky bottle giving Bloor and the tea a wide berth.

'And how long a sentence have you been given on Cable and Wireless hill, Hanrahan?' Sir Henry noticed Terry Hanrahan was still swaying slightly.

'Six weeks for me, too. Special project upgrading the Federation satellite network. But I may stay longer. Wait for them to build an airport.'

'And what's this upgrading going to give us? Something sensible like Channel 4 racing?' Hanrahan accepted the offered whisky because the tea obviously wasn't working.

'Nothing as exciting as that, Ambassador. In fact rather the opposite. We're putting in a new state of the art satellite blocker. The upside is that you'll be the only people in the whole world who won't have to watch Home and Away. Instead they're going to be beaming you Fed. TV.'

'And what, in the name of Rupert Murdoch and all that is holy, is Fed. TV?'

'Sorry, not my department. All I do is stick the wires in the holes. Or at least I hope I'll be able to when my hands stop shaking. But whatever it is it's apparently coming from some American base in Cuba.'

'Well if there's nothing on TV,' said Bloor, tiring of Lady Ethne's detailed progress through the troubled genealogy of the Nunburnholmes, 'is there anything that passes for a decent hostelry in Jamestown?'

'The Consulate hotel, the White Horse and The Standard and,

to my knowledge, none have won the pub of the year award even though they were the only entries,' said Jardine with feeling. 'The Standard's a corrugated iron shed where you'll find the nearest thing Jamestown has to ladies of the night but they're probably blind drunk by eleven in the morning and you'd certainly not survive the trip to hospital in Capetown if you went anywhere near them. The White Horse is the locals' knocking shop and The Consulate is Fawlty Towers with termites. And just to top off their dubious charms they're all technically off limits to incoming staff and firmly covered by the Federation Official Secrets Act.'

Hanrahan realised there was something to be said for being stuck on Cable and Wireless Hill and Theodore Bloor made a mental note to visit all three watering holes at the earliest opportunity.

***

Donald Reeves hadn't been looking forward to Birtwistle being dumped on him. Jardine had made the excuse the British Embassy was full. He'd then turned the knife by saying a steady British brigadier might be able to talk some sense into his tank happy American officers. The American Ambassador had been in a John Wayne sulk for a week since Jardine had ambushed him at the Joint Staffs meeting and his mood had been made even worse when he reported the spat to Rumsfeld. The Secretary of Defense had been characteristically blunt, suggesting that Reeves was losing the plot.

More worrying still, he'd casually mentioned that there could shortly be a vacancy in Belize? As if St. Helena wasn't bad enough. He'd only just persuaded Dee to come here, twelve hundred miles from the nearest shopping mall. He'd never get her to Belize with its white mans grave climate and a guerrilla war thrown in.

Reeves worst suspicions about too clever by half senior British officers were confirmed when Birtwistle the bluff breezed off the boat and strolled through the security gates at the pier head. In the manner of giving beads and mirrors to the natives he'd somehow managed to lay hands on a bouquet which a starched young lieutenant presented to Mrs. Reeves.

'I suppose by rights at this point I should offer greetings from Her Britannic Majesty but by the oversight of some incompetent courtier they forgot to invite me to the Palace to pick them up before I left. So good morning from Birtwistle is all I can manage I'm afraid.'

'We done stand on ceremony here Mr. Birtwistle.' Said Donald Reeves sharply. 'Just try to do a professional job. British protocols permitting.'

'So this is sunny Jamestown on Sea.' Birtwhistle, ignored the little barb and looked out over the heads of the crowd jostling on the quay. 'It looks peaceful enough this morning. Even quaint if you half close your eyes.'

'Yeh, but you Brits. have always had a soft spot for anything that sniffs of the tail end of empire.'

Birtwistle, eyes shaded from the fierce sun, scanned the two rows of sagging and peeling houses that made up Jamestown Main Street and thought that scragg end of Empire would be a more appropriate phrase.

'The place looks as if Kenneth More or Peter O'Toole would be more use than an off the shelf brigadier. Or maybe Ronald Reagan would be more your style?' He beamed in Reeves' direction and mimed drawing his six gun but Reeves didn't seem to appreciate the joke. Suit yourself, thought Birtwistle. 'You've got to admit the place does look like a bit like a B movie set waiting for a spaghetti western to ride through.'

Reeves looked at the extras crowding the pier head. 'We've certainly got a cast Hollywood would die for, Brigadier. But before you meet them I think we'd better get you a proper briefing. But only if that doesn't get in the way of your sightseeing of course.'

A truck arrived to pick up the junior officers and their equipment and Birtwistle set off behind Reeves on the short walk to Castle Hall. Outside the Consulate Hotel a group of Saints were noisily playing cards on the dusty steps amongst sawn off petrol drums full of plants displaying various symptoms of impending death. The street market that stretched up to The Standard was a

54

cacophony of hawkers and caged poultry and braying donkeys tied to trees. Mingling with it all was the sound of a gospel choir drifting from one of the abundance of chapels that seemed to cater for every obscure shade of Pentecostal religion. The sounds were compressed and amplified by the walls of rock that towered either side of the narrow street. Birtwistle stopped and looked up to the bouldered rim etched sharp against the sky.

'Yeh, that's a problem,' said Reeves following his gaze. 'Rocks peel off regular. Most of them land in the empty lots behind the houses but some go right on through. While back one went right down through a bedroom takin' a baby with it. The mother was sleeping easy in the same bed and wasn't touched. Not a scratch.'

Outside a little grey building that announced itself rather grandly as the St Helena Central Library founded by Governor Wilks in 1813, Birtwistle spotted a stone memorial IN MEMORY OF NINE PERSONS KILLED BY THE FALL OF 1500 TONS OF ROCK. APRIL 1890.

At Castle Hall the Ambassador turned in between the two armed Marines on guard duty and once the double doors with their etched windows swung to the sounds of the film set subsided. Birtwistle checked the ornate Victorian ceiling for signs of boulder damage.

Reeves loped off down a dark corridor and knocked briskly on a door graced with a faded coat of arms and KEEPER OF THE REGALIA in chipped gold paint. Florence Lacey's office was a strange mixture of the ancient and the tacky. Its floor to ceiling shelves were filled with polished leather bound volumes but on the desk was a vase of plastic flowers. Above the empty fireplace was an oil portrait of what looked like an African warrior chief receiving homage from a group of white explorers but beside the grate was a chair filled to overflowing with multicoloured cuddly toys.

'Briefing, Miss Lacey. Brigadier needs brought up to speed fore he gallops off to start his reevue.' As Donald Reeves trotted out of the office it occurred to Birtwistle that this was a man he probably didn't want to do business with. Judging by the look of mild distaste which flickered behind Florence Lacey's perched spectacles she evidently felt rather the same. The cowboy boots clattered away down the corridor.

'Long time since there was a galloping Brigadier, Miss Lacey. Boer War like as not.'

'Well that's as good a place as any to start. That's the last time the Island was so busy. Six thousand Boer prisoners in 1900. But that was before the typhoid got a grip and wiped a lot of them out at Deadwood Camp.'

'And if Ambassador Reeves wanted to go there he would presumably ride the Deadwood Stage.' Birtwistle thought he'd better make the most of their bit of common ground.

'Yes and I'm Doris Day.' Florence Lacey lit a cigarette as she pretended a stern look over her spectacles. 'But perhaps we should get down to some serious work.' She unfolded a map on the desk. 'This is the lie of the land at the moment but it's all about to change. Liberia on the coast with the Central African Republic to the east of it and Uganda further south.' Birtwistle was no longer thinking about the silliness of Donald Reeves; nor yet about Florence Lacey's cloying perfume which, until a moment before, had been reminding him of school holidays with a particularly unpleasant auntie in Eastbourne. 'Then it gets complicated. In the far south we've had to make space for Zimbabwe and Republika Srpska – that's the Serb bit of Bosnia Herzegovina...'

'Radovan Karadzic.'

'Very good. You're obviously a fast learner Brigadier.'

'They stopped emptying the prisons to staff the army some years ago.'

'I must have missed that edition of The Times.'

Birtwistle wasn't entirely sure if Florence Lacey was being first division insulting or fourth division coquettish. 'But Karadzic is still on the run; still wanted by the War Crimes Commission in The Hague. Isn't he?'

'Ah. The very first thing to understand about The Colony, Brigadier, is that, in such relations as it has with the rest of the world, things are rarely as they're reported and hardly ever as they seem.'

'You mean they're not reported and, if everything goes according to plan, they stay out of sight and out of mind.'

'More or less. At least until the political expediencies of The Federation require another course of action.'

'Which translates as…' Birtwistle paused and ran his finger over the map '…we're running a colony here that half the world doesn't know about.'

'Oh, much more than half. In fact only Britain, America, France and South Africa officially know we're here. And very few politicians in any of those countries know the details.'

'So we've got a secret colony that we're slowly filling up with.. what should we call them? Political prisoners, troublemakers, terrorists? '

'No, Guantanamo's for terrorists. Here we keep dictators.'

'Dictators that the rest of the world thinks are somewhere else, if not dead, and all the while they're being happy campers out here at Butlins, St. Helena?'

'Good shot, Brigadier, except we now suspect they're not quite such happy campers as we thought they were. There's even the suggestion that a couple of them are perhaps planning to disrupt the prize bingo.'

Birtwistle was beginning to think his time on the island might not be quite such a boring paper push after all.

'Not that any of them are going anywhere. There are only two ways in and out of the colony.' She leaned over the map again. 'The only deep water harbour is here in Jamestown and the only ships allowed to use that are the mail boat that brought you down, our regular Tinsley supply ship and occasional Royal Navy boats. Tight security whenever there's a ship in. We also have the option of a long range helicopter link from Cape Town but it has armed air marshals on board and lands in a secure compound on Ladder Hill."

Birtwistle pushed port and airport security to the top of his list.

'Not everyone here has a one way ticket of course. Circumstances change. As we speak it's been decided that Qadaffi is our new bulwark against Islamic extremism rather than a sponsor of terrorists. Easy mistake to make. So we're getting ready to send him home from a place he's never been.'

'And you'll make sure his mouth is so full of money he can't tell the world about your little holiday haven.'

'You're going to do *very* well here, Brigadier. In fact I think it's fair to say you've picked up more since you got off the boat than Reeves has managed to grasp in the six months he's been here. Anyhow, that's not your problem. We have another category of guest, too. We call them non territorials. They're here, how shall we put it...in sheltered accommodation as it were. You're quite likely to bump into some of then in Jamestown and I'm sure you'll recognise them when you do. But please don't stare. They get frightfully touchy.' Ignoring Birtwistle's rather quizzical smile Miss Lacey swept her finger round the south west coast of the island. 'But the big developments are going on here. The Federation is about to expand its sphere of influence and we expect to have to accommodate anything up to six new Sovereignties. Which, after an altogether too long preamble, is why you're here. The fact of the matter is we'd been reluctant to expand until we got the existing territories on a more stable footing. Unfortunately London has taken a rather different view and we now hear that at least two new guests, complete with assorted hangers on, will be here within the week. Hence the need for your security review. Drink?'

'Do you think we've time for one?'

'Oh, however pressing the business, in the heat of Jamestown, Brigadier, one has to keep one's levels up.' Florence reached into a desk drawer and brought out a bottle of scotch and two glasses. 'And I'm sure you'll still be fit for the boat trip to Cape Town tomorrow when you can get a flavour of the way we do things here.'

'So what I'm having now is just a spot of shore leave.'

'Yes, you'll be sailing on the St. Helena at noon, weather permitting, with the Jardines – Sir Henry, British Ambassador and his wife – as a sort of welcoming party.'

'And the object of our attentions?'

'Need to know basis, Brigadier. I'm sure Sir Henry will fill you in at the appropriate time. He may even mention the rather delicate matter that the Americans don't know about some of the expansion plans.'

'Ah,' said Birtwistle, 'so you'd rather I didn't include any of this in my small talk over the burgers and ketchup when I'm playing Tonto to Ambassador Reeves' Lone Ranger.'

'Quite. And since you raise the point, just remember that Tonto had called the Lone Ranger Keemosabe for all of seventeen television series before our hero realised it meant horse's arse. As I say, things aren't always as they seem.'

'Hey, ho silver,' said Birtwistle smiling broadly and pushing his empty glass across the desk.

'I fear we won't be able to keep the Americans in the dark for quite so long as that, but I think it better that, in the meantime, Ambassador Reeves continues to believe your visit is a very British waste of time and money; that you're a surplus to requirements Brigadier that's been sent here to do an entirely superficial report about aspects of cross border security. A report which of course will be given careful scrutiny by the powers that be on its short trip to the waste paper basket.'

While she poured, Birtwhistle leaned closer to look at the map and pointed to two shaded patches in the island interior. 'And what are these areas?'

Florence Lacey settled back in her chair and the top button on her blouse succumbed to the pressure. Following Birtwistle's eyes she glanced down but made no attempt to fasten it. 'The Colony may be controlled by the Federation –Britain and the US in effect, but there are some other foreign interests in the place too.' A finger encrusted with startling nail varnish pointed. 'That one there is South African. They still maintain the Boer cemeteries at Deadwood. And you've got to remember that, despite us having the most interesting telephone directory in the world, most of the work here is really pretty routine –a bit of cheap and cheerful diplomacy to keep our international partners on board and a fair amount of ego-polishing for our residents.'

'But do the ones with territory really believe they're still running the place?' His hand came to rest on Uganda.

'Now that's a question better left unasked, we find, because if you do ask it you start to let inconvenient chinks of light into corners best kept as obscure as possible.'

'You mean they're all barmy.'

'In the world of international politics, Brigadier, one has to be ever so careful how one sets the parameters of lunacy. You've no idea who you might catch if you get it just the teeniest bit wrong.'

'So Margaret Thatcher isn't with you - yet?'

'We have enough to be going on with.' Said Florence smiling wryly and topping up Birtwistle's glass with a measure of scotch that would have had Denis Thatcher raising an eyebrow. 'But to get back to practicalities and to finish off the grand tour, this area of up country is officially a Department of France. And they take it very seriously, resident Consul, the works. In fact they're the only other country to keep a 'guest' here. Remember Baby Doc Duvalier? Course you do. Took over from his dad in Haiti. Robbed the place blind. Among his particularly nasty little scams was selling Haitian cadavers to American medical students. Anyhow, eventually the Pope went to Haiti and told them to get their act together so Baby Doc had to high tail it to France. Gave up the corpse trade so far as we know but still got to be a bit of an embarrassment – living it up in Cannes, buying Chateaux and Ferraris and generally being the disreputable playboy. So they shipped him here. And this is a nice touch. They keep him in the house at Longwood where the nasty Brits. kept Napoleon Bonaparte prisoner until he died. Or was murdered.'

She paused briefly to let the idea sink in. 'And that...' – another stab of the fingernail '...that is the Emperor's grave.'

CHAPTER SIX

Tony Blair brooded by the window and looked down on the cream of the political press being whipped into action by John Prescott's antics in the street below. He'd emerged from the Ministerial car with a brown paper bag over his head.

'No truth in the rumour you're in bother again then John.' Shouted Harry Warren the underworked chief political correspondent of the Daily Star.

Even after all his years as Prime Minister, Blair never ceased to be amazed at how news of committee squabbles managed to get back to Downing Street before he did. He made a mental note to get Alistair Campbell to arrange a spot of ministerial phone tapping again. Prescott peeled off the bag to reveal a broad smile. 'Thought it was a different kind of tit you specialised in Harry.' Then having checked that the radio and telly crews were out of earshot sheltering from the drizzle. 'Maybe you should persuade Kathy Perkins from the Sun to get her kit off – 'WEAPONS OF MASS SEDUCTION- WHAT A PAIR OF BAZOOKAS' – I can see the headline now.'

'So you're not here for a carpeting?' Shouted Miss Perkins leaning forward over the barrier and revealing a hint of the two reasons she'd got the job.

"Ah, there you are, Kathy. Nae, lass we've got the whips office for that sort of thing, but you can carpet me anytime.' A ripple of applause from the press corps as Prescott persuaded the cheery policeman on duty outside Number 10 to take a bow with him and model the paper bag. 'And next time you hear me going on about the Wapping whoppers you'll know I'm not talking about your editor's habit of telling porkies.' A cheer rising from the street sent Blair to his desk as Prescott whistled into the office without knocking.

'No business like show business then John?' His voice crackled like ice on a pond.

'Just keeping the enemy sweet Tony,' as he threw himself into an armchair by the desk. 'Somebody has to after Campbell's been biting their ankles. Anyhowoff you look as if you've got a problem.'

'No, on the contrary, I think it's you who's got the problem, John. Particularly as, after consideration, I've decided that things can't go on as they are.'

'We'll be sorry to lose you, Tone. Except for Gordon of course. Make the porridge gobbler's day. But I should be keeping my voice down. He's probably got a glass against the wall in Number Eleven listening to every word we say.'

Voice raised now. 'Then he'll be able to hear me telling you that I'm sick and tired of you playing the fool. I don't know what you're up to with your little asides about the Federation and Liberia and the Central African Republic but on the basis that it's marginally preferable – just marginally mind you - to have you inside the tent pissing out I've decided to have a little re-shuffle...'

'Not sure Mrs Prescott would like Chequers. Too much hoovering....'

'...I'm taking you off regional affairs and giving responsibility for them to Margaret Beckett...'

'Well she probably can't make more of an arse of them than she did of agriculture – except I suppose your average councillor doesn't get foot and mouth....'

'And I'm also taking the opportunity to get rid of Claire Short before she has another of her sanctimonious flounces about...'

'Now *she'd* be good at running farming – mad cow. It would be like putting down her relatives....'

'I'm offering Claire a punishment cell on the distant back benches and giving you her old job at Overseas Development.'

The curtain came down on John Prescott's music hall act.

'No, you can't be serious. You're making me Handout Harry?'

'I'm sure you'll have them rolling in the aisles in Ethiopia and The Sudan.'

Prescott's jowls deepened and there was an uncharacteristic silence.

'And the deputy PM job?'

'Don't sulk, John, you can hang on to that. We all know it was never more than a sop to the wild and woollies in the unions anyway. So for the time being you can carry on pretending to be Tony's socialist conscience.'

Prescott perked up. Rebel without a cause had always suited him.

'And, yes before you ask. You can keep the flat.'

The chuckle came back to his chin.

'But so far as the Overseas Development job is concerned you're going to be working out of the Foreign Secretary's office. That way he'll be able to keep an eye on you. Check you're so on message that you'll feel you've got your vibrating pager up your arse – to borrow a phrase from the Prescott dictionary of quotations.'

'I thought you had to mug little old ladies in the street to get a sentence like that.'

'Take it or leave it, John. There's always a spare seat next to Claire Short.'

***

From: < rev.taylor@liberiaweb.com>
To: < emperor@centralafricanrepublic.gov>
    <bigdaddy@uganda.gov>
Subject: party
Date: Mon. 10th February

Blessings from the Rev. Spoken Big Daddy. Welcome home party Jamestown 25th suggest. Fix Americans good. Can Bok travel? Diplomatics sorted. Trade mission agreed. Chuckie prays for us.

From: emperor@centralafricanrepublic.gov
To: <rev.taylor@liberiaweb.com>
    <bigdaddy@uganda.gov>
Subject: party
Date: Imperial calendar confirms

D'Accord. Have 2 come overland. Bangui aeroport temp.closed. Waiting spares release France. Have you contact number for Medicine Sans Frontieres. Christ be protect you. Bokassa.

63

From: <bigdaddy@uganda.gov>
To: <rev.taylor@liberiaweb.com>
  < bok.emp@centralafricanrepublic.gov>
Date: 11th February
Subject: Men of powa party
Good hear. Amin sorted Britannic Majesty so no problem come 25th. Go easy mitta Christ. Allah strong guy big field marshall fella. Need billet Presidential Guard. Nothin fancy hospitalitywise. Heinz tomato soup wid do. Hasbe Heinz. Quartermastr Intrim govment let run out. Hangin in trees now. Nobody run out soup tomorrow. cu 25th. If time I cure Bok sickness. King of Scotland.

Terry Hanrahan's computer bleeped a warning and the exchange of emails flashed onto his security screen. Code Red. The boredom of the surveillance shift lifted. He'd not had a Code Red since he arrived in the whispering silence of the Cable and Wireless communications centre. He read them again – soup and prayers, sickness and things hanging in the trees. But the cryptographers would no doubt spot something that he couldn't. He checked the operations manual. The mails were on the Colony loop so not venturing into any bit of cyberspace more than twenty miles from where he sat. But Code Red required instant report to Security Ops. in Jamestown. He downloaded them into secure storage and looked up the duty number. That afternoon it was listed as American Embassy, Ambassador's secure channel. He dialled.

'Reeves.'

'Hanrahan at Cable & Wireless, Ambassador. We've got a Code Red email exchange. They're in your file 10/2/FY653.'

Reeves scrolled through them on screen. 'Yee-ess!'

'Yes, you've got them?'

'Yes, I'm going to boil the Jardine's airs and fucking graces in tomayto soup.'

Perhaps psychiatrist rather than cryptographer, thought Hanrahan as Reeves slammed down the phone.

***

The Jardines and Birtwistle, having just finished lunch in their hotel at Cape Town International Airport, strolled out onto the balcony to watch the Air Zimbabwe jet touch down and taxi away from the terminal towards a parking area on the perimeter. The flight wasn't announced on the airport's arrival screens. Jardine was leafing through the Cape Argus.

'It seems things are going to be rather easier for our lords and masters at the Nigerian summit after all, Brigadier. Poor Mr. Mugabe seems to have taken a turn for the worse and apparently has been given special dispensation to fly to England for urgent medical attention.' He turned to the editorial page. 'There's even speculation that he may be so poorly it will be a one way trip.'

'Yes, a free and well informed press is such a civilising influence, don't you agree dear said Ethne looking up from the fashion pages.

'And what about number two?' Asked Jardine.

'Due down in about twenty minutes if it's on schedule.' Birtwistle glanced up to the arrivals screen but immediately realised that flight wouldn't be listed either.

'Good. Time for a snifter before we go then. As we're going to be spending the next twelve hours practicing our bedside manner and playing happy bloody families.'

Half an hour later as their car approached a hangar in the furthest corner of the freight area a Boeing 757 stripped of all paint and markings and shimmering in the afternoon sun landed on the emergency runway and taxied to a halt beside the Air Zimbabwe jet.

'CIA Air making themselves unobtrusive again I see,' said Lady Ethne twitching a smile in Birtwistle's direction and smoothing away the hint of a crease from her skirt.

A lounging squad of South African Special Forces stood in the shadow of the hangar, unseen by the plane spotters on the terminal roof who were frantically trying to identify the unmarked plane in their well thumbed copies of World Airlines Review.

'The Zimbabwe contingent first then.' Birtwistle unfolded himself from the car and strolled across to the red carpeted disembarkation steps. As he climbed towards the open door a toy pram rolled out of the plane and tumbled towards him. A little girl wearing a bright floral patterned dress and with hair in pigtails scampered after it. Three or four steps from the top she lost her footing and took flight. The Brigadier caught the pram in one hand and scooped up the little girl in his other arm. Looking up he saw who he took to be the girl's mother, Grace Mugabe, hand to her mouth and beside her the dapper but sour figure of the man his detractors call Robert the Brute.

'Well caught, sir.' He said as if he was in the members' enclosure at Lords. Mugabe's voice had a strangely metallic ring to it.

'Welcome to Cape Town transit, Mr President,' said Birtwistle, setting down the squirming bundle of floral dress who clambered back up the stairs to hide behind her mother's skirt. 'Perhaps you'd care to follow me to Immigration clearance.'

'My husband doesn't do immigration,' said Grace sharply. 'And as he's unwell I expect him to be treated with humanity as well as respect.'

'Minor formalities concerning your attendants and advisors which we'll expedite with all speed. Nothing more. And if you'd like assistance, Mr. President, I'm sure I could organise medical orderlies and a stretcher.'

'Now....' Mugabe paused as if collecting his thoughts. '...we mustn't allow silly rumours to start, must we? It wouldn't be in any of our interests for people to think that 'Hitler' has lost his grip. Would it?' He slowly made his way down the stairs leaning heavily on his wife's arm. Air Zimbabwe obviously didn't supply complimentary, in flight copies of the Cape Argus.

The youngest Mugabe insisted on pushing her pram. A string of sheeted airport trailers loaded down with the considerable Presidential baggage preceded them to the hangar. Above the open doors was the sign FEDERATION AIRWAYS MAINTENANCE. Several small aircraft were in bits inside being worked on by men from RAF Regiment who could rebuild and dismantle them with their eyes shut having done it so many times before. Birtwistle led the small

Presidential party past the armed engineers who studiously ignored them and through another door into the transit lounge which could have been a VIP suite in any modern airport in the world. Sir Henry read out the brief but flowery formal welcome and ushered Mr. Mugabe to a sofa. Behind it, crossed Zimbabwean flags framed a portrait of the President in happier times. The Presidential doctor fussed with his bag which opened out into something approaching a mobile field hospital and Lady Ethne was in animated conversation with the President's wife about the horrors of the Imelda Marcos shoe collection – something she'd discovered over the years was universally despised no matter how comprehensively the people she was talking to had robbed their own National Exchequer. A blur of floral dresses and shirts marked the passage of the Mugabe's three children.

Sir Henry nodded to Birtwistle who set off to collect their other passenger. As the brigadier walked out onto the shimmering tarmac the Air Zimbabwe jet was slowly taxiing away towards the terminal, presumably to the delight of the group of weary passengers whose flight to Harare had been delayed for twenty four hours due to what had been variously described as bad weather, essential maintenance and unforeseen circumstances.

Birtwistle shaded his eyes against the glare reflecting from the gleaming bare metal of the unmarked aircraft. In the one patch of darkness made by the open forward door he could just make a small, solitary, black figure, the sun glinting from his round spectacles. Birtwistle stopped at the foot of the steps and the man began to walk down towards him. His progress was accompanied by a strange slapping sound. The sole of one of his shoes was hanging off. As he came closer, Birtwistle could see that his expensive suit was frayed at the cuffs and that his starched white shirt had grey smudging round the collar. He stopped when he was a couple of yards from the Brigadier.

'And where have you brought me now?' There was resignation in his voice.

'This is Cape Town transit, Mr. President. Welcome.'

'Then you'll have to forgive me, sir, if I repeat the speech I've already made at Port au Prince, Bangui, Johannesburg and Jamaica.'

He paused and wiped his spectacles then looked clear into Birtwistle's eyes.

'My removal from office as elected President is unconstitutional and illegal under international law.'

His English was slightly stilted and with a strange, exotic, heat of the afternoon lilt.

'I have not resigned, as my opponents have suggested. In fact I've been kidnapped by an alliance of American and French forces and twice flown half way round the world. My constituency is the poor people of my country and I've been removed because I dared to claim back the $21 billion that the French authorities have stolen from us by supporting brutal dictatorships and generations of slavery. I also oppose continued American exploitation of our natural resources and their clandestine backing for the one per cent of our population that owns eighty five per cent of our nation's wealth. I protest at my treatment and demand that I am returned to my country and my Presidential duties forthwith.....'

His voice faded away into a sigh as if he'd made the speech so many times that even he was bored with it.

'I'll make sure your protest is officially noted, Mr. President.' Birtwistle couldn't square the image of the slight, silent figure in front of him with the stories that had preceded him; stories of excess, corruption and the eating of babies.

'If you'd like to follow me, sir.'

Jean-Bertrand Aristide, philosopher, priest, accomplished musician and linguist, deposed President of Haiti, the poorest country in the western hemisphere, flapped along behind the brigadier towards the transit lounge. Once inside he sat quietly, his battered cardboard suitcase by his feet, his hands folded in his lap, ignoring the chaos of Mugabe children that ran around him.

'Ladies and gentlemen your onward transport is ready for boarding.' Birtwistle stood silhouetted in the door at the back of the hanger and fractured beams of sunlight played across the highly polished floor with every small movement he made. 'Perhaps President Mugabe and his family would like to board first.'

Robert Mugabe was helped up from the sofa by his doctor and after a moment's pause in which he seemed to be restoring his equilibrium, he walked straight- backed to the door. Outside a Chinook helicopter squatted like an offensive insect by the perimeter taxiway. The Mugabes were escorted to the front of the aircraft. President Aristide, limping like an injured bird, was shown to a seat in the rear. Between these two little areas of sovereign space was a curtained cabin for the Ambassador's party and two surly and heavily armed Federation Air Marshals who seemed to have taken a vow of silence.

'I suppose a drink and a hand of cards is out of the question,' said Sir Henry to no-one in particular as he strapped himself in. Momo conjured a bottle of Glenlivet from his pocket, Ethne Jardine found cards in her handbag and Birtwistle laid hands on a supply of RAF issue plastic cups.

The British captain who sounded rather like the star of a Pinewood romantic comedy of the 1940s gushed onto the intercom to explain that the flight would take approximately eight hours, that the weather en route was generally good and that a Tri-Star tanker would rendezvous with them in mid ocean to refuel them in the air which he thought would be an experience they would all find jolly fascinating.

'Bloody nonsense,' muttered Sir Henry half filling a cup. 'Just fly the bloody aeroplane.'

With a vibrating and lumbering roar the Chinook rose above the hangar to the delight of the plane spotters and banked to the west out to sea.

CHAPTER SEVEN

Theo Bloor was taking the air and enjoying the bustle of Main Street. With the Jardines away he'd found himself rattling round the Embassy and needed company. He'd already had a couple of steadying cans of beer in the Standard, hemmed in by a press of drunks and their thrumming chorus of belching, out of tune singing and snoring. What he hadn't spotted were any of the ladies of the night promised by Sir Henry. Maybe the Consulate Hotel would come up trumps. He brushed away a beggar and the bead seller who took his place and stopped by one of the market stalls to watch a couple of fishermen carving up what he took to be a tuna. It already smelled past its sell by date. His stomach churned.

'You want?' said a girl who'd appeared out of the crowd.

Remembering what Jardine had said about the ladies of Jamestown Bloor checked her over. She looked sober even though it was past eleven in the morning. And pretty with a dark olive skin and wild black hair that fell below her shoulders. The notion of a young Carmen came to mind as he glanced down to the part laced bodice of her faded dress.

'I want – what exactly?' The edge still taken off temptation by Sir Henry's government health warning.

'Well I don do Rolex watches or ditty poscards.'

'So what exactly do you do?'

'You stranger on yown. I show you Jamestun.'

'Well that shouldn't take long.'

'Drink first maybe to get quainted.'

Bloor, ever confident of the antiseptic and medicinal properties of alcohol if taken in sufficient quantities, took no further persuasion. 'And where do you suggest? I don't think I can manage The Standard again. Much as I want to soak up the atmosphere its spittoons were just rather too brim full of local colour.'

'We go Whytorse, this way.' She led on occasionally stopping to check that Bloor was still with her. She took him past a potato and yam shop selling its wares by the gallon. Past a chemist with cobwebbed carboys of coloured liquids in the window that looked as if they'd been evaporating for a hundred years. Later Bloor would find out that this first reaction wasn't far off the mark. The shop had been established by a chemist at the time of the Boer War and the present owner had altogether forgotten what the carboys contained. The woman turned into a little square off Main Street where an old man sat slumped against one of the ornate metal pillars of a market canopy and ever so slowly played an asthmatic accordion. Bloor stopped to listen to him and the black haired girl came back to reel him in. 'Whytorse ovear.' She took him by the wrist and pushed on through the crowd.

The bar of The White Horse was emptier and brighter than The Standard. It had chintz table cloths – albeit rather grubby ones. Groups of men huddled in corners and there was a low hum of conversation. Theo ordered a beer; his companion 'vodkatonk'.

'Room?' said the barman as casually as if offering a bag of crisps.

'Certainly not,' said Bloor, shirtily. The haughty effect he intended was rather spoiled as a mouthful of beer went down the wrong way and he spluttered over the bar.

'Mebbay' said the girl quietly, leading Theo to a table at the empty end of the room. As he sat down he glanced past her to the other customers to see if any of them had registered that hint of a promise. None of them was taking any notice.

'So waseyname?'

Odd, though. He was sure he knew a couple of them; vaguely recognised them even though he couldn't immediately put names to the faces.

'Hey, waseyname?' She tried again, laying her hand on his arm.
'Theo. Theo Bloor.'
'Sounds Sathefrican.'
'Nothing so exotic. Just boring old roast beef English for

generations and generations. And you?'

'Ahna. From Jamestun for genrations and genrations.'

'So, as I asked before, what do you do, Ahna?'

'Yousay.'

'Well that could take quite a long time with someone as pretty as you.'

Bloor's greasy attempt at gallantry was interrupted by a squabble that had broken out at the other end of the bar and Bloor glanced across, momentarily diverted from the business that was about to be in hand. The barman moved in to calm things down and Ahna took Bloor's arm.

'Lessmove. Quietplace.' As the dispute began to subside she led the way to a staircase behind the bar, along a shady upper corridor and into a room flooded with sunlight and with a view of the market square. Theo looked down at the jostling crowds and above the hubbub of voices could just hear the wheezing accordion. Then it was drowned out by a pounding roar that rattled the window frame and a shadow fell across the room. The helicopter flew low over Jamestown and banked away to the north.

'Independence Day,' said Bloor, slipping out of his braces and watching the shadow ripple away across the rooftops. 'And I think we should celebrate it young lady.'

But when he turned Ahna had gone and in her place, sitting on the edge of the lumpy bed, was a squat man in crisply ironed military fatigues. Bloor's eyes darted from the man to the door and back again.

'My apologies for the lil ception, but I thought was best we meet away from prying eyes, Meester. Bloor. I will send Ahna back when we've talked. If you still want.' The man's voice had a strange, jarring edge to it like a cheap clock about to chime.

Bloor quickly slid into his braces and picked up his jacket from the chair. He knew the face in front of him. Pockmarked by acne and with a permanent hint of an ironic smile. But for the life of him he couldn't put a name to that face.

'And why, precisely, do you want to talk to me in secret?'

Asked Bloor, regaining some of his composure.
'Because it will be mutually beneficial, simple as that.'
And then it came to him. The acne that had given the man the nickname of Pineapple Face – but not said to that face if you wanted to survive for long. The officer stood and held out his hand.
'Manuel Noriega. Pleasure to meet you, Meester Bloor.'
The pleasure obviously wasn't reciprocated judging by the clamminess of Bloor's unwilling and limp handshake.
'If you keep abreast of world affairs, which I'm sure you do, you will know that I am presently in a Florida jail serving a very long sentence for drug offences.' He smiled, creasing the pockmarks into dimples.
Bloor was regaining his blustery composure and he remembered bits and pieces of the story - that Noriega had been deposed as ruler of Panama by an American invasion, that he'd holed up in the Vatican Embassy in Panama City and that the Americans got him out by playing amplified rock music outside his window for some days. That he'd apparently worked for the CIA for many years and that the head of one of his political opponents had been found in a US postal mailing sack. That wasn't a comforting thought at this precise moment. Then he remembered that Noriega had supposedly had a religious conversion in prison. Which was.
'I see you do remember. Or at least you remember, maybe, the officially sanctioned versions of events.'
'Well this certainly doesn't look like a prison in Florida.'
'Well done, Meester Bloor."
'But I still don't know what we can possibly have to talk about.'
'Illegal sex. It would be as good a place to start as any…'
Bloor wilted.
'A number of girls who are a liddle too young and whose rather sordid tales have come to the attention of some of my….associates.' Noriega reached into a pocket and brought out a handful of photographs which he laid on the bed. 'And of course it's our wish that the officially sanctioned image of Meester Bloor as an

upstanding and talented writer and artist be protected.'

'And who are these…associates of yours?'

'Let's just say people who need certain information they feel you might be able to provide.'

'Doesn't blackmail sit rather uncomfortably with your religious conversion, Mr. Noriega?'

'No, such a coarse word, blackmail.' Noriega looked genuinely distressed.

'I prefer to say that I am working for a greater good.'

'And what information could I possibly have that would bring that greater good about?'

'I'm merely a humble messenger, you understand. But my associates believe that the British authorities – and you are presently their honoured guest – may be engaged in some, how shall we put it, sleight of hand.'

'You want me to spy on the Embassy. Out of the question.'

'I agree. It would be a wholly unacceptable breach of trust. And we would never consider asking you to do such a thing. But conversation, social intercourse, snippets overheard. What harm could there possibly be in noting such things. Particularly if they referred to harbours or container ships or new residents. And if there's no harm how can you possibly object.'

Bloor glanced down at the photographs.

'And even if it *does* offend your sensitive nature, Meester Bloor,' a note of distaste crept into his voice. 'How can you possibly object?'

The fat man said nothing as he put the pictures in his pocket.

'So maybe time to call Ahna back.'

'Oh, I don't think I have the stamina for that anymore.'

'I'm sorry to have spoiled your afternoon delights, Meester Bloor, but I'm sure she'll be able to find you when you have something to report and then perhaps you could carry on from where you left off, so to speak.'

At the door Noriega turned.

'Ah, and it may be of help to know that the Charge d'Affaires at the Embassy, Pike I believe he's called, has his own liddle peccadilloes. Rather different from yours, of course. His indiscretions involve the American Ambassador's wife. Rumour has it that they go swimming together..' Noriega mimed the breaststroke. 'But of course that may be code for something rather more energetic.'

***

Ambassador Reeves paced about among the weeds growing through cracks in the concrete pad on Ladder Hill as he waited for the Chinook to come in. The uniforms of the armed marines guarding the gates of the compound were dark with sweat. Pike sat on an empty oil drum by the tin shed fanning himself with his panama. Someone had scrawled the word 'ARRIVALS' in chalk on the door of a large corrugated iron shed. DEPARTURES was presumably still in the planning stage. The bandsmen dozed in the shade of a clump of almond trees, worn out by having to get to grips with two national anthems in one morning. The guard of honour had just finished setting up two temporary flagpoles, neither of them straight and another soldier hoisted the national flags while Florence Lacey fussed with her paperwork.

Statues had been dispensed with on this occasion because Aristide had been something of a surprise visitor and they didn't have one of him in stock. They did have a Papa Doc Duvalier in the warehouse and the American Ambassador had initially argued that one failed Haitian dictator was very much like another, ignoring Pike's protests that Aristide had actually been an implacable opponent of the Duvalier regime. But eventually even Reeves had to accept that the Papa Doc statue with its distinctive, funereal frock coat, top hat and an outstretched hand holding a voodoo-sacrificed cockerel was a bit specific.

They heard the aircraft before they saw it. Pike and Reeves shaded their eyes to the north east. A few seconds later the Chinook banked into view round Flagstaff Hill and flew low over Jamestown scattering the seabirds. As it came in to land the Chinook's downdraught blew away the band's sheet music leaving them stuck in an orchestral no man's land somewhere between Zimbabwe and Haiti. Whatever it was they were playing obviously wasn't recognised by any of the passengers as they walked towards the rattling tin sheets of the arrivals hall. Sir Henry and Lady Ethne marched ahead and Birtwistle manned the green line between the nations. The armed air marshals posed Rambo like at the helicopter door to repel boarders and as soon as the passengers were at a safe distance the dipping rotors wound into life and the Chinook clattered away to meet its refuelling aircraft.

Pike shouted the formal greetings over the noise of the engines. Sir Henry waved in the vehicles from where they were parked in the shade. Reeves' armoured limo (shipped in as deck cargo after it became too tatty for Presidential cavalcade duties) and an American military truck would take the Mugabes across the border to Harare. They needed the truck because they had a pile of luggage which looked as if it probably contained the Zimbabwean national debt. An army Landover, improbably camouflaged with waving greenery which made it look remarkably like an army Landover run amok in a sugar cane plantation had been requisitioned to transport President Aristide and his one small, battered suitcase on the shorter trip to the Consulate Hotel.

The moment the last door slammed Reeves rounded on the Jardines.

'So much for your goddam meddling.' He waved an email print out in front of Sir Henry's face. It might have been the SP of the 4.30 at Cheltenham for all Jardine could see of it. His quizzical look sent Reeves into overdrive. 'Yuv jeppadised the security of the colony. Yuv encouraged a reevolt. Yuv broken every rule in the goddam book. Yuv....'

'I think we've been experimenting with the bourbon again Ambassador,' said Lady Ethne, making it sound like a biscuit. 'Do let's get down to what's what.'

'Because of your ill advised ex-periment with amateur deeplomacy we've got an insurrection on our hands. That's what.' Pushing the emails into Sir Henry's hand.

Even when he'd read them they still didn't mean a lot.

'May I?' Asked Lady Ethne, who was rather more au fait with the mysteries of cyberspace, having corresponded by email from various postings around the world with her sister in Goring on Thames.

'I think your wife has caused quite enough problems already.'

'I do think one should have ones blood pressure checked Ambassador. I don't think your alarming colour can entirely be put down to the effects of the sun. But have no fear. No need to trouble yourself further. All we have here is a silly party invitation.'

'THEY'RE PLOTTING AN UPRISIN'.' So loud now that even President Aristide looked up from his reverie in the motorised sugar cane thicket.

'AMIN'S THREATENIN' TO FIX US..'

Sir Henry turned to Pike who was smiling rather stupidly. He'd been passing the time by imagining the top of Reeves' head exploding in a particularly colourful way...

'What is Ambassador Reeves ranting about?'

... and then the gallant Pike helping his not-so-grieving widow from the graveside to..

'Pike.'

...the comfort of a four poster bed in a nearby ...

'PIKE.'

...hotel.

'PIKE.'

'Sorry. Sorry sir. Been a long day. You were saying?'

'A long day? Unlike you Pike I've just spent eight hours in a bloody paraffin budgie that was marginally more cramped than the average carriage on the Northern Line at rush hour. I'd hoped that if God spared me, which for a while when we were bouncing around on a hosepipe from a bloody petrol tanker doing aerobatics I doubted – I'd hoped, harboured the slenderest of ambitions, that I might get back in one piece to the colony – NOT A BLOODY MADHOUSE. So I was just saying. What's. Going. On?

The whisper more ominous than the shout.

'Apparently C and W picked up some emails which I must say I thought were fairly innocuous. Just assumed they'd got their Code Red settings in a stramash again.'

'Hevyall taken leave of your senses?' Reeves was striving to match the sinister qualities of Sir Henry's whispering but ended up sounding more like Hoagie Carmichael. 'What we got here is three unstable doolallys planning organised resistance.'

'As you can tell, Sir Henry,' said Pike 'in your absence Ambassador Reeves and I have taken marginally different positions on the matter.'

'Code Red is Code Red. No argumentation.' Reeves was coming back to working pressure and Sir Henry was losing the will to live. Pike, meanwhile, was getting into his stride.

'Except you'll perhaps remember the embarrassing little business two years ago, Sir Henry – before your time Nr. Reeves - when their high tech machinery, or whatever it is they use, set off a full scale hoo-ha. It mixed up the CIA with C&A. It turned out that some junior from Cable and Wireless was trying to rustle up a party suit by mail order.'

'From C&A? A combination of disbelief at the habits of the common people and twenty minutes in the baking sun had taken Lady Ethne to the end of her notoriously short tether.

'But this aint suits. This is big trouble brewing you take my word for it. We're talking tyrants here who've already blown away God knows how many thousandsa people. They aint gonna stop at a few more here.'

'What a vivid imagination you do have, Ambassador Reeves. In my personal experience, as I've felt it necessary to tell you on an earlier occasion, Charles Taylor has been perfectly reasonable in his demands during his stay with us –the odd social visit, a trade delegation here and there. Keeps him believing he's still doing his day job. Emperor Bokassa, meanwhile, is a sick old man scarcely capable of dressing himself, let alone leading a frenzied attack and President Amin is renowned, in British corridors of power at least, for his wicked sense of humour.'

78

'I don't give a plugged nickel for the British corriodors of power. Washington wants all three of them put in seecure custody and that's come from Rumsfeld himself.'

Sir Henry snapped. 'Unfortunately Mr Rumsfeld is neither here nor in charge. Next time he's in London he can complain to the Prime Minister, he can complain to the Queen, he can complain to the bloody Coca Cola Company for all I care. He can have me sacked. He can have me transferred to Afghanistan. He can make a model of me out of waffles and maple syrup and stick pins in it if he so chooses. But in the meantime, until the Joint Staffs business is sorted out, I'm in charge of security and my decision is to let Brigadier Birtwistle carry out his review before we start filling up the Jamestown jail.'

'I've already had Amin de-tained.'

It was the turn of Sir Henry's face to run through the Dulux shade card to Imperial Vermillion. 'Did you know about this pike?'

'Fraid not, sir. Too busy with today's arrangements.'

Jardine was now so close to Reeves he could smell his breath freshener. 'I should have you chained up in the next cell. No, on second thoughts, the same cell. Having first let President Amin know that you are not only homosexual and masochist but also Jewish.' His thin smile was not a comfort to the American Ambassador.

Sir Henry turned away as if from an infestation of maggots.

'I'll go with the Mugabes, assuming they haven't already fried to death in the car. Pike will travel with Aristide and drop Lady Jardine off on the way. Birtwistle – you'd better hitch a lift with Miss Lacey. I'm afraid there'll be a slight delay on the security review while you arm yourself with a get-out-of-jail-free card and liberate President Amin. Pikc will join you to take him back to Kampala – trying manfully not to generate any further international incidents. And I'm afraid you'll have to find your own way home, Ambassador. Momo – go with him, discourage him from making any further arrests on the way and if you happen to have any homicidal thoughts – for God's sake don't resist the temptation.'

The convoy bumped away down a rutted track, dust turning the sky red in its wake as it hung in the breathless air. Reeves stood watching them go then kicked a stone which clanged against the wall of the arrivals hall. After a few minutes he flounced off, Momo in tow, towards The Ladder – 699 precarious steps down the face of the hill into the centre of Jamestown.

***

'And who built that?' Birtwistle was looking up at The Ladder from Florence's car as they approached the Harbour Square.

'Royal Engineers in the 1820s as a quick way of getting to the gun emplacements on the top.'

'Doesn't look very quick to me.' They spotted Reeves and Momo, still only about half way down. Even at this distance Birtwistle fancied he could see steam coming from the Ambassador's ears.

Miss Lacey's car, which Birtwistle thought smelt rather like the perfume department of a provincial department store, wheeled round the square and through the archway leading to the insignificant little building that served as Jamestown prison.

'I'd imagined something more substantial.'

'Oh, no need for it most of the time. Despite the exotic inmates there's hardly any crime here and what there is will usually be among the locals. Bit of drunk and incapable, odd family punch up about who's having who. Fact is there's nothing to pinch and nowhere to hide it if you do. No, our dear little colony makes your average British village look like Sodom and Gomorrah. Here a single lady can feel safe on the streets.'

The tiniest emphasis on 'single' encouraged Birtwistle to head for the safety of the streets. But once free of the car the noises coming from the prison suggested Florence Lacey was being rather too charitable about the joys of downtown St. Helena. He stepped through the open door of the prison office as a chunk of porcelain toilet bowl exploded against a wall and showered a desk. Beneath it a man wearing what Birtwistle took to be the uniform of warder knelt with his hands over his head. The Brigadier craned round the

80

corner of the door towards a row of cells which looked as if they could once have played host to Butch Cassidy and the Sundance Kid. Four out of five of them were occupied by men who appeared to be either dead drunk or just dead. But the middle cell looked as if it had suffered a neutron bomb attack. A burst mattress and shredded sheets stuck through bent bars. Splintered furniture littered the floor. Water fountained from the jagged remains of the dismembered sink. And in the middle of it all stood a beaming figure who, in the dim light, could have passed for a larger than life Curtley Ambrose as he picked up another chunk of dismembered sanitary ware and bowled it at the warder's middle stump.

'Howzat,' said Birtwistle. 'Well bowled Mr President. And perfect timing. I do believe it's the tea interval.'

Amin put on his uniform jacket, straightened his cap and waited while Birtwistle took the keys from the cowering warder and made to unlock the cell door. Faced with the threat of Amin unbound the warder made a break for the street. Amin, though, was demonstrating the Pavlovian reaction to senior British army officers that had marked his rise from village urchin to despot. They may have regarded him as a buffoon and sniggered behind his back; they may have told stories about him that enlivened many a King's African Rifles mess dinner. But behind it all there was an understanding. They were equals to the extent that they could do each other a favour.

'Marybon Cricket Club limp wrist shower compared Ugandaside. England only robbed World Series reason Queen bribed umpires.'

'Quite, Mr. President.' Birtwistle was trying to ease the twisted door.

'Different be next time I'm captain...' He took strike using a remnant of bed frame as a bat. '...and Field Marshal.' A deep chuckle started somewhere by Amin's gleaming boots and rolled up through him. The barred door gave way to Birtwistle's pressure with the help of a clout from an armoured and polished toecap and the Butcher of Uganda strolled, flexing, from the cell as if leading his team from the visitors' dressing room.

81

There being no sign of Pike, Birtwistle decided that tea was a safer alternative to allowing Amin to roam the streets. He stopped by Miss Lacey's car and told her to send Pike on to the Consulate Hotel if he ever deigned to turn up. As they strolled out to Main Street Amin asked him which number wife was that. He said he hoped the others were more prettified. Relishing the thought of the emasculation Miss Lacey might have wrought had she heard the comment, Birtwistle confined himself to suggesting the British Army must be thoroughly old fashioned because for some unaccountable reason they frowned on sending even one wife as a helpmate on active service.

'Uganda Army no silly women rules. I want my officers be active, active every which way. Keeping things strong moralewise you get fella?' He mimed 'active' in a way that instantly cut through the language barrier. The crowds parted like the Sea of Mecca. Men Saints watched the grand uniform pass by and laughed at the joke. Women Saints tut tutted. Then they, too, laughed and sidled up to their menfolk. Babies would be made that hot afternoon. Some of them spares.

The two big men climbed the steps and went in through the elaborate doorway of the Consulate Hotel and, as if emerging from a time machine, they were suddenly in what Birtwistle remembered as 1950's Eastbourne. The only things missing were Max Jaffa's Palm Court Orchestra and the Brigadier's overperfumed auntie. The potted palms were still there dustily sulking in corners. Customers looking like the extras from a Noel Coward film whispered at tables with starched white cloths and tiered cake stands. Local waitresses corseted into black and white uniforms scurried their silver service. A gangling and obsequious waiter appeared as if by magic from behind a palm.

'May I find you a table, gentlemen?'
'Table here close by door and back gainst wall for me settled.' Amin glared.
'I'm afraid...' spoken as if mucus had been given voice '....I'm afraid that particular table is taken. As you can see.'

82

'Untake it. Pronto maybe, before you closed up.'

The manager swallowed hard and somehow managed to smile insincerely at the same time taking on the look of a bemused iguana. The old gentleman, dozing at the table, snorted and stirred as Amin eased himself into the tight grip of a vacant chair. Birtwistle shrugged, sat beside him and ordered tea and scones.

'Strawberry jam or blackcurrant?'

'Dundee stuff mamalade. No nancy English jam.'

'I'm afraid....'

'You be fraid mister. No Dundee stuff you maybe jam yoself when they finding you.'

The old gentleman woke up with a start and pulled his dressing gown tight around him. Seeing a Field Marshal and a Brigadier across the table, the stuff of his dreams came alive and he was once again in his glory days at a meeting of the Junta.

'Reports of Marxist insurgents Valparaiso, Chiquita, Morador.' Spoken in the sort of accent B feature Nazis who've escaped to South America use.

'We dispose of them.'

Despite the worsening security situation the waiter sidled in regardless. 'My sincerest apologies, General Pinochet, I hope you didn't mind me offering two fellow officers a place at your table.'

The General waved the iguana away and whispered closer to Birtwistle. 'Bad idea civilians eavesdropping on military discussions. That's why Allende was such a fool. He let civilians take charge, make the decisions. Recipe for disaster.' He shuffled even closer and lay his hand on the Brigadier's arm. 'There are dangerous men on the loose. Round them up. Dispose of them.'

Try as he might Birtwistle couldn't think of a single thing in his army training that covered this eventuality. So he fell back on the manners of the mess. 'By the way, sir, may I introduce President Amin of Uganda?'

'And is that President for life?' Asked Pinochet.

Odd question, thought Birtwistle.

'President for whose life?' Amin chuckled. 'It's President much

I want it be.'

'And this, I surmise, is General Pinochet from Chile.' Said Birtwistle, extending a hand which was studied intently by the general and then ignored.

'Augusto Pinochet Ugarte -Commander in Chief, Professor of War, elected President. At your service.' Somewhere under the table a pair of heels clicked. Or they would have done if they hadn't been wearing carpet slippers.

'Elected Presdent.' Amin was obviously struggling with the concept. 'OK make people love you so want kiss yo ass. Tell dem Big Daddy loves em too, maybe. But go easy numbers game. Too much people can count these days.' He mimed counting on his fat fingers.

'My life's work has been for the people and for Democracy herself,' Pinochet growled, looking at Amin with some distaste. A flutter of newspaper cuttings drifted past Birtwistle's mind's eye documenting the democratic blood letting and torture that followed Pinochet's overthrow of the Marxist President Allende sometime in the 1970s.

Pinochet warmed to his own defence like someone who's had much practice. He turned to Birtwistle. 'The English and I have much in common, yes? Mrs. Thatcher and I have much in common, yes?'

'These are dangerous deep waters for an ordinary soldier, Mr President.'

'But sometimes an ordinary soldier like me, like you, has to save his country, yes?'

'Old fashioned as it may seem we've tended to leave it to the politicians to do that sort of thing,' Birtwistle offered.

But the P word didn't play well with either Pinochet or Amin who suddenly seemed to have found some common, broken ground. Voices were raised. The argy bargy about corrupt politicians, self serving politicians, incompetent politicians, weak politicians went on for some minutes. People round the room were beginning to look up from their lethargy of tea and scones. After a while Birtwistle grudgingly started to think his companions may just have a point.

'So you want a politician.' Pinochet had got a second wind and cut through the brouhaha. 'Clement Atlee was a politician, No? Clement Atlee was a democrat, No? And what did Clement Atlee say?'

'If it moves – nationalise it. I think,' said Birtwistle, trying to lighten things up.

'Clement Atlee said 'Democracy is government by discussion. But it only works if from time to time you can make the people shut up'.'

Pinochet's voice rose and rose and when he stopped the whole room was silent.

Birtwistle grappled for a moment with the surreal concept of Pinochet taking Clem Atlee as his mentor but was brought back to earth by a kafuffle beside the front door.

'I will not be quiet.' President Aristide stood in the doorway.

'And I will not share a roof with those men.' He was pointing a wavering finger in the direction of Amin and Pinochet. 'A fascist general and an Islamist tyrant.'

The Islamist word brought Amin back from his finger counting. He'd reached eight. 'Maybe I show him power of Allah break arms so can he only point floor direction.'

'I think, perhaps we'll leave it to Mr. Pike,' Birtwistle intervened. 'It would be such a shame to get blood on your splendid uniform. Blood's so difficult to get out my mother used to tell me.'

'She obviously didn't have enough practice,' Pinochet mumbled, drifting off again, tired out by chairing the long meeting of the Junta. Meanwhile, Pike was calming Aristide with the promise that Amin and Pinochet were merely passing through. The lizard was summoned to show the President to his apartments. As they were leaving, a Creole woman with vast acreages of chest undulating freely under a starched white tent came across the room at speed and gathered Pinochet up from the table.

"ChikichikiMedicinetimetoilettime." Her high pitched and singsong voice seemed to belong to another body. The General, too,

85

was shuffled away with very little protest. Pike beckoned to Birtwistle.

'I think I should get President Amin home to Kampala, if that's OK.'

'And just when I was starting to enjoy the party, Mr. Pike. But to keep Ambassador Reeves happy shouldn't we make Amin turn his pockets out before he goes just in case he's been nicking the hotel cutlery?'

'I think the odd fork and teaspoon is a small price to pay for keeping the international peace.'

'But it is peculiar isn't it. Amin doesn't seem at all upset. In fact he looks as if he's quite enjoying himself too.'

'Why shouldn't he? Gets him out. Takes the edge off the boredom. And he knows as well as we do it's not the real world.'

He turned to go and then looked back.

'I think.'

Amin whistled as he strolled across the lobby towards them, juggling a jar of marmalade from hand to hand. As he took his leave of Birtwistle he checked Pike wasn't listening and said, 'Nurse lady too damn good chilly whatshisname. You send her do bed bath shift Kampala. Big Daddy get bouncy bouncy. Brigadier get V.C.' And he winked an elephant eye as he ambled away.

CHAPTER EIGHT

Prescott would be Caliban to the Foreign Secretary's Prospero. At least that's what the Foreign Secretary was thinking as he glided up the grand staircase of the Foreign and Commonwealth Office on the morning the new Minister for Overseas Development was due to start his job.

'But he probably thinks the Caliban run Afghanistan.' He chortled out loud to the mild surprise of the cleaner who was polishing the banisters.

'Morning guvnor.'

He responded by running a manicured finger through imaginary dust.

'Hear the Mouth of the Humber's starting this morning. Good lad, John. E'll rattle things up a bit,' said the headsquared lady winking into the burnished brass.

The Foreign Secretary stopped in his tracks and his head turned towards her as if on a ratchet. 'Most dreadfully sorry, Mrs char. Didn't have you down as PHD in political philosophy material – more GNVQ 1 in hoovering. And judging by this carpet – failed.' He moved onwards and upwards, a statue on castors and, having set the tone for the day, relished the prospect of the honed sarcasms he could unleash on his minions.

In contrast, the Honourable Member for Hull East was joy itself when, a quarter of an hour later, he ambled into the hallway and almost tripped over the cleaner's bucket.

'How you doing, Annie? You used to be- where was it - Environment when I last fell over your kit?'

'Yeh, but couldn't stand Marsham Street. All that 'orrible concrete. Just couldn't get it clean. So got promotion to a better class of staircase.'

'Anyoff good to see you girl – who's in?'

87

'Lord and master. Usual sarky mood.'

'Better go and pull his chain of office then.' He headed for the stairs. 'By the way don't agree about the staircase. Looks like the entrance to a Turkish brothel.'

'Wouldn't know. Never had the luck to clean in a Turkish brothel. Probably better tips.'

Prescott chuckled and headed up the stairs and the cleaner shouted after him. 'Oh, by the way, talkin' about foreign parts. If he starts going on about Caliban and Prospero don't for gawd's sake even mention Afghanistan.'

'You what?'

'Prospero. Just remember he's the Duke of Milan and Caliban's the fat bloke he nicked an island from. Shakespeare. The Tempest.'

'You been at the brass polish?'

'Just a bit of insider advice.'

'Didn't have you down as a PHD in English Literature, Annie.'

'Don't you start.'

As Prescott wandered along the first floor corridor he heard a burst of laughter coming from one of the Under Secretary's offices.

'You know old matelot Prescott used to be a steward on Cunard line. So he knows the world – well he once saw the Hook of Holland through the second class dining room window. Great training for Overseas Development Secretary.'

The laughter erupted again as he moved towards the door.

'And last week when Prescott was standing in at PMQs, Fatty Soames shouted across the Chamber, *a whisky and soda for me, Giovanni and a gin and tonic for my friend.*' Another burst of laughter as the head of Prescott appeared round the door.

'And mine's a pint of Tetleys.'

The laughter abruptly stopped. The head disappeared and re-appeared.

'And I'll have the Tinsley Shipping files on my desk in twenty minutes if you lot don't want to be seeing the world through the job centre window.'

Prescott found the Foreign Secretary sitting alone in the

overcooked grandeur of the Durbar Court reading the morning papers. He came here every working morning to connect with the spirits of great Foreign Secretaries past. Men who still had an Empire to run rather than the sadly diminished chain of corner shops for which he was responsible. But at least here he still had the trappings of Empire unlike so many of his Ambassadorial staff around the world who were working out of rented offices in gloomy suburbs or even out of a laptop in their back bedroom. He blamed the decline on the grasping entrepreneurs who'd run the treasury ever since the 'grocer's daughter' days of Margaret Thatcher.

'Ah, John. Welcome to your new posting. Just reading a very interesting article about Caliban.'

'I'll have you know I've lost seven pounds in three weeks. Pauline's got me on some diet where I can only drink water and eat millet that I always thought was for budgies. I've told her for a birthday present I'm expecting a mirror and a swing.'

'Are you feeling well John?'

'Caliban. The fat bloke that had his island nicked by the Duke of Milan or some such. Shakespeare. The Tempest. You weren't mixing him up with them headbangers as run Afghanistan were you?' Prescott made a mental note to slip Annie a bottle of gin. May be she'd let him have a snifter to take the edge off the millet.

But His Excellency didn't look best pleased. 'Ye-es, interesting as it is, John, to hear of your extensive knowledge of everything from our feathered friends to Shakespeare and international terrorism I fear there's work to do. I've of course arranged for your office to give you an extensive briefing ...'

(Get me up to the hocks in rainforests of reports that nobody else has ever bothered to read, translated Prescott.)

'....And we've organised a number of low key familiarisation visits.....'

(Get me out of the country to some hell hole at the end of a dirt track where the mobile phone doesn't work.)

'....And after the debacle with Ms Short we've appointed a new lady advisor to your department who's been tasked with establishing well managed media relations...'

(Some Blair's babe from the Downing Street thought police who'll try to stick to me like shit to a blanket.)

'....And last but not least, John, the Cabinet Secretary has decided to attach one of his most trusted lieutenants to your office to make sure you toe the line.'

'I think you translated that one for me...'

The Foreign Secretary allowed himself the flicker of a smile.

'But with all these spooks about,' said Prescott, 'will there be a space for me to lay my weary red box? Maybe I should work from home.'

(Yes he's going to try to beat the system, translated the Foreign Secretary. Well, just let him have a go. But in his own, oh so common, vernacular we've got him tied up tighter than a duck's arse – and that's watertight.)

'Oh, I think not John, I think not. Good Morning.'

***

'What a bloody awful day.'

Sir Henry slumped into an armchair and Lady Ethne's hand, bearing a bloody awful day measure of black label, was immediately in place to allow the swift and efficient transfer of vital fluids.

'Not sure who's worse,' said Jardine, holding out the empty glass for a refill, 'Mugabe himself or that jumped up secretary wife of his. She made a real bloody song and dance about the size of the bungalow.'

'Well they always do, dear. Bit of a come down from what they're used to when they no longer have a national exchequer as a piggy bank. And they'll calm down when Pike takes them to see Zimbabwe House under construction. Just make sure that this time he gets the workmen to take down the Bokassa Imperial Palace banner or whatever it was they left up when Amin got the guided tour.'

'And what about Aristide?'

'Apparently he's locked himself in his room and is refusing to talk to anyone but George Bush.'

'Obviously no bloody taste then.'

'Now, Henry, we mustn't let our little personal prejudices cast a shadow over the Special Relationship, must we. But talking of personal prejudices, dear, it wasn't possible to put it off any longer. I'm afraid Mr. Bloor is about to join us for dinner.'

Sir Henry sunk deeper into his chair. 'No, that's beyond the call of duty, Ethne. Dictators and the deranged I can cope with. Mass murderers and international pariahs, all part of a day's work. At least they're usually interesting – although I suspect President Aristide is going to let us down badly in that department. But a boring bigmouth with BO is too bloody much.'

'And an undiplomatic alliteration too far, if I may say so, Henry. But never fear. I'll put him at Pike's end of the table. He can waft his unpleasantnesses down there.'

Jardine didn't look convinced.

'And just to get all the bed news out of the way at once, Henry, I'm afraid it's General Noriega's turn to be guest of honour. But as you seem to have taken a sudden liking to the humanitarianly inadequate you presumably won't mind him sitting next to you.'

'Apart from a face that looks like a suntanned golfball, that he washes in an aftershave that can paralyse the senses at fifty paces and his constant boasts about how bloody proficient he is in the erection department, he's just the perfect dinner guest.'

'And it could be President Bokassa's turn. At least the staff won't have to get unsavoury stains out of the dining room carpet.'

An hour later, Jardine had balanced his fluids so successfully that he was giving a passable, if rather unsteady, impersonation of a host who was actually pleased to see Theodore Bloor. And as ever, Lady Ethne was on hand with the diplomatic sticking plaster.

'Mr. Bloor, Henry and I are so, so sorry to have had to leave you to your own devices in the past few days but I do so hope that Momo and the staff have been taking care of your every little need during our absence.'

'Splendidly, Lady Ethne, splendidly. But then your staff have obviously been trained by a consummate professional.'

Perhaps it was the greasy residue of the remark that helped Lady Jardine to glide so effortlessly across the room, on her way to introduce Bloor to Mrs Reeves. She'd come alone because her husband was still sulking in his ambassadorial depths and plotting ever more painful ways of bringing Sir Henry's career, if not his life, to an end. As she did her introductions it occurred to Lady Jardine that there was such a pleasant symmetry in putting the two worst dressed people in the room together. Bloor, looking like a gone to seed Oscar Wilde, sporting a bookie's hanky tied in a bow and bursting out of a stained dinner jacket with more shine than knap. Dee Reeves bursting out of a dress that looked as if it had been run up out of a set of Odeon cinema curtains and cut so low she scarcely dared breathe, let alone move.

So this was the blousey, pouting subject of Mr. Pike's attentions, thought Bloor. After Lady Jardine drifted away, a couple of minutes of the lady's one sided conversation that ranged far and wide from shopping to the lack of it in Jamestown, persuaded Bloor that if information was to be gleaned this was just the empty head from which to extract it.

'I do believe we share an interest, Mrs. Reeves.'

'Oh ahm sure we do Mr. Bloo-er, but what particular interest did you have in mind.'

'Swimming, Mrs. Reeves. The great freedom. Giving ourselves up to the vast, comforting bosom of the ocean.' She glanced down, proudly.

May God forgive me, he thought.

'You're right.' She clapped her hands and a wave of perfume overwhelmed Bloor's natural aromas. 'You're just sohw right. It's my most favourite thing in the whole waiyed world and how clever of you to realahse.' She sounded like a southern belle who'd somehow managed to escape from a Tennessee Williams play.

'And I understand that a mutual acquaintance, Mr. Pike isn't it, knows just the place to go to find the best swimming in the whole Colony.'

'Now how did you know that?' She jiggled. 'Has some notty boy been telling tales outa school?'

'Can't remember where I heard it, dear lady. Just that somebody mentioned the best place is close to a harbour somewhere up country.'

Demonstrating a better sense of timing than he'd ever shown on official duties, Pike arrived on the scene just as the word 'harbour' sailed over Bloor's lips and his usual pleasure at the sight of Dee Reeves in all her glory was dashed.

'Mr. Bloor, couldn't help overhearing. Must be a misunderstanding because of course there isn't a harbour up country.' He was gabbling like Peter O'Sullivan in the final furlong.

'Av course there is,' chuckled Mrs Reeves making an ill advised turn to starboard that threatened to bring down the cinema curtains. 'Where was that big ship going if there isn't a harbour, silly. You remember the one with all the sailors that waved to us.'

Pike almost choked on a canapé and Bloor thought that this spying business wasn't anywhere near as difficult as John Le Carre had made it out to be. But then Momo announced the arrival of the guest of honour and as General Noriega made his entrance and smiled in Bloor's direction the cockiness suddenly evaporated.

***

Terry Hanrahan walked down from the squat concrete bunker that was the Cable and Wireless monitoring centre to the garden of Longwood House. In a tight shuttered room at Longwood Napoleon Boneparte had drawn out his long, final days in cancerous or poisonous agony, depending on which version of the tale you believed.

Hanrahan had been spending many of his off duty hours in the musty library at Longwood, there being little else to do but sleep, wander the scrubby hills or join the interminable poker school that seemed to run twenty four hours a day in the C and W mess. And Napoleon's story was certainly more exciting than any of that. Yesterday he'd turned up a yellowed report in the archive which told how news of Napoleon's death had arrived at Plymouth in 1821, many months after the event. A young captain had ridden day and night to take the news to George 1V. When he was shown into the King's presence he cried 'Sire, your greatest enemy is dead.' The King, thinking at that moment about his unwanted Queen, exclaimed 'Is she by God, I did not even know she was ill.'

Hanrahan smiled again as he leaned back on a broken, rustic seat and soaked up the intensity of the light after his long shift in front of the insipid green screens of the monitoring station. This corner of the garden was where Napoleon had a see-saw built. A see-saw. With nobody on the other end. His last, failed balancing act. Here he made a new Empire in his head and towards the end he scarcely noticed that he was powerless and frail. One of his gaolers said that having created an imaginary France and an imaginary Spain, here Napoleon – the stripped Emperor– set about creating an imaginary St. Helena as well.

'Lovely afternoon, isn't it. Quite reminds me of the hills above Cannes. Similar light.' A tall, dark skinned, lumpy man dressed in a white linen suit and sporting L shaped side burns had emerged from the shrubbery. 'You don't by any chance have a cigarette, do you?'

There was the slightest hint of a French accent.

'No, sorry. Don't smoke.'

'Pity.' The man stretched out a small hand that looked out of proportion to the rest of his body. 'Jean-Claude Duvalier. I'm the naughty house guest and the French authorities are looking after my health. No booze, no cigs. They don't want me popping off prematurely like a certain earlier inmate.' He smiled broadly.

'Terry Hanrahan, Cable and Wireless. So how long have you been here?'

'Just over two years. I think. Days do so drag when ones gratifications are limited. It could be less.'

'And how long will you be staying?'

'Now that's a question I can't get an answer to however many cockerels I slaughter.' Another disarming smile. The Duvaliers were reputed to be the high priests of voodoo, Hanrahan remembered from some magazine article he'd once read in a dentist's waiting room. 'Mind you, the pins stuck in the doll have given the French Consul a nasty head cold, a rotten toothache and a bad back in the last few weeks. Only joking.'

Hanrahan looked into Baby Doc's sparkling eyes and thought he'd reserve judgement on that. But it not being every day that he ran across a fully functioning dictator, his curiosity got the better of him. In the absence of Napoleon himself, Duvalier would have to do.

'But what would you do if you could leave? Apart from the cigs and the booze, of course.'

The lumpy man was suddenly serious.

'Live up to my responsibilities, of course. Become the head of the family again.' He made it sound as if he was talking about the Mafia, thought Hanrahan.

'Go back to Haiti?'

'Probably not straight away. Don't think they're quite ready for me yet. But they will be. Eventually. When all the democrats and do gooders have made a complete mess of things and the communists have crept in and people realise that they miss the strong man. They may not like him and they may not like everything he does. But they like the certainty. They like to know what's what.'

Duvalier's face, like an animated cartoon, switched from frown to grin.

"Anyhow, shouldn't be talking shop on a lovely afternoon like this.' He turned to go and then stopped. 'Oh, and if you did manage to smuggle in a packet of cigs or a bottle of decent brandy – even a bottle of indecent brandy would do – you could be a member of the Ordre Royal et Militaire de Saint Henri in next to no time. Much cheaper than Honours in England and no awkward questions asked.'

Duvalier crashed away into the undergrowth and Hanrahan imagined he heard the sound of a strangled cockerel. He sat smiling for a while before taking his usual route across to Hutt Gate at the head of the path that led down to Napoleon's tomb. Blue butterflies slowly unfolded and folded in the shade of the hedge. There was an incessant croaking from the frogs that live by the spring which used to provided Napoleon's drinking water at Longwood. And then he was through the gate and back into French territory; a little amphitheatre bounded by hibiscus. And around the simple white tomb agapanthus and nasturtium. The willow trees he'd seen in some of the early prints had gone, though. Apparently visitors to the island had taken rather too many souvenir cuttings and the trees died. It's said that a tree grown from one of those cuttings can still be found in Bournemouth and Hanrahan had made a note to go and see it.

He knew the tomb was empty. Napoleon's remains were eventually taken back to France and reburied in some splendour. Well, most of his remains. Hanrahan had read in the Longwood library that the cancer which supposedly killed him was preserved in a glass jar in the Royal College of Surgeons' Museum in London. He didn't think he'd bother looking that up when he went home.

He hadn't noticed the figure by the tomb at first. It startled him when it moved, when it seemed to unfold out of the vault with its arm across its chest. He'd read that a freed slave woman used to sit here and for a few pennies would recite doggerel verses about the disinterment of the Emperor to any visiting pilgrim. But he was sure she wouldn't have been dressed like this.

'Sorry if I spooked you,' she said throatily as she sat up. Florence Lacey's bikini was hugely patriotic, each triangle sporting the Union Flag, but in all other practical respects it was inadequate. 'I was just communing with history. And normally you never see a soul up here. Such a pleasant change from the crashing and banging of Jamestown.' As she sat back on the white tomb two of the little flags threatened to unfurl.

'Sorry to interrupt your communing.'

'Lacey. Florence Lacey.' She shot out a hand for Hanrahan to shake.

'Rejoice in the title Keeper of the Regalia. Sounds like something straight out of Mervyn Peake, doesn't it. Which I suppose is appropriate on this Gormenghastly island.'

'Terry Hanrahan.' As they shook hands the flags waved.

She glanced down, following Harahan's look, and smiled.

'Vexillology.'

He looked up. 'Sorry?'

'Vexillology – the study of flags. And I do believe you've gone pink, Mr. Hanrahan.'

'So how long have you been on the island?' At a flustered stammer. 'As I was saying to President Duvalier just a few minutes ago.'

'Ah, you've met him. He always seems to me a bit soft centred, a bit limp wristed to be a murderous tyrant. What did you make of him?'

'He seemed jolly enough. Tried to scrounge a packet of cigarettes, but then I don't have many tyrants to compare him with.'

'Oh, they're all very different. The biggest mistake in our line of work would be to suggest they all came out of the same mould. They'd be horrified at the thought. Nobody claims to despise tyranny more than tyrants. Individually they really do think they're the good guys, wilfully misunderstood by the nasty Joint Powers. They always think they're running their bit just fine, it's the rest of the world that's going to hell in a hand cart.'

'So how long have you been keeping the regalia, whatever that may mean?'

'Massaging egos. Keeping up appearances. We don't want them getting uppity.'

Hanrahan was still none the wiser.

'Three years. In fact I've done longer than most of the 'guests'. The difference is I was daft enough to volunteer.' Never taking her eyes from his face she slowly reached back and untied the bikini string behind her neck. The two flags fell away. 'Would you be very sweet and rub on some sun cream?'

She rolled onto her stomach and lay across the white slab of the tomb.

Maybe the two weeks of hell on the RMS St Helena were worth it after all, he thought, as he reached for the bottle of lotion. He worked silently for a few minutes and when he was finished Florence rolled over and propped herself up on one elbow. "I've got

97

a little confession to make, Terry. You don't mind me calling you Terry? This meeting isn't entirely accidental. I'd heard from somebody at C and W that you tend to come down here in the afternoons and I was particularly keen to meet you in private.'

'Don't tell me. Because I've got soft hands.'

'Well, that too. But to be absolutely honest I took rather a fancy to you when I saw you come off the boat. I was doing the diplomatic bag run that day. I know you looked a bit green round the gills but we aren't exactly spoiled for choice in the fresh faces department.'

Hanrahan laughed and the frogs went quiet for a minute.

'Oops, I could probably have put that better, couldn't I?' She smiled broadly and sat up on the edge of the tomb. 'What I meant was that recycled conversation is the curse of colonial life.'

'Oh I don't think I'll bear a grudge.'

'Good. Because I think we could probably help each other in a number of ways.'

'I think you'd better be a bit more specific, Miss Lacey.'

'Florence. Oh, do come and sit down. You're making the place look untidy. The fact is there are certain things happening here in the Colony and about to happen, more to the point, that I need to explore.' Another, more confidential smile. 'And you, being the very clever technician you are, would be just the person to keep me – how shall I put it - abreast of things.'

'There's the minor matter of the Federation Official Secrets Act.'

'And there's white mischief. But we're both on the same side, Mr Hanrahan. The Act hardly applies to our conversations. Particularly as I'm making a kind of informal, unofficial, official request on behalf of Her Britannic Majesty's Government.'

It occurred to Hanrahan that things probably wouldn't have turned out like this if the job had been in St Helens.

'But, Terry, before we talk any more about those minor matters, it's a lovely afternoon and we have the place to ourselves and I think it would be a terrible shame if we didn't make the most of it, don't you?'

Several times in the next half hour Terry Hanrahan thought it was just as well Napoleon had been dug up and sent back to France because he most certainly wouldn't have approved of this new use for his old tomb. Or maybe he would.

CHAPTER NINE

John Prescott sat in his new office surrounded by heaps of document boxes and reports. They'd been arriving for two days. So many of them that nobody noticed the few marked 'Tinsley Shipping'. He'd ignored the reports on Ethiopian aid programmes and investment in Sub Saharan Africa. He put to one side case studies on earthquakes in Turkey and Tsunami relief. But, try as he might, he still couldn't make any sense of the Tinsley papers. He'd set into them with a vengeance when the six boxes arrived from the archive but by the time he'd got to box two he'd ground to a halt in a mire of manifests and requisitions. There were shiploads of building and construction equipment. There was what looked like a giant grocery list – half a container of Heinz tomato soup, another of Dundee marmalade, cases of Talisker and Black Label. There was one tantalising reference to imported statues being shipped from the Balkans and North Africa. Even stranger was a special, one off consignment of bagpipe equipment. The porridge gobblers, having taken over Britain, were obviously now taking over the world, thought Prescott.

But what was lacking in the paperwork was any rhyme or reason. The final destination for all these shipments was never mentioned although he assumed it was a certain mid Atlantic island. But he hadn't been able to find a single reference to what was going on there or why these strange cargoes were being shipped half way across the world.

But then in the third box, tucked into a sheaf of papers dealing with bulk cement cargoes he came across a note marked 'Classified', written by an under secretary at the Foreign and Commonwealth Office and, presumably, misfiled.

'Yes!'

His Downing Street minder popped her head round the door.

'Something you need, Mr. Prescott?'

'No, Harriet, still got plenty to be going on with. Just can't put these reports down.'

'I'm glad you're finding the new job so interesting. Always knew you would.' Of course she knew no such thing but at least he was still working in his office where she could keep an eye on him and listen in to his calls.

'Any chance of the guardroom rustling up a cuppa?'

When she'd gone he slid the papers from under his red box.

CLASSIFIED
From: Blount FCO
To: Head of Strategic Development - Federation
Subject: Code 1 cargo

New harbour at Turks Cap has taken its first Tinsley delivery and so far as we know Reeves and co are still in the dark about it. There was a bit of a scare last week but Jardine seems to be keeping the lid on things. We're doing what we can to muddy the waters by stringing out the current Joint Staffs dispute in Liberia- that was a bit of luck - but Reeves is raging and Washington can't be too heavy with him for obvious reasons. Main consignment still due on the 25th weather permitting. RN will be shadowing and will make the ship day at Jamestown coincide.

Tinsley have moved the main construction crew down to Tristan and the ODA port project there will keep them out of contact for at least two months so we have some breathing space.

Prescott sat back in the ministerial chair with his hands behind his head and realised he was still as much in the dark as Reeves – whoever Reeves may be – but at least he now had a bit of paper which he reckoned might make a bit of a splash if he ever dropped it in the pond. But he'd hold off doing that. In the meantime the note had given him one or two little phrases which, even if he hadn't the faintest idea what they meant, might bring an uncomfortable spark of recognition to the eyes of the enemy.

Harriet the minder arrived back with the tea in Prescott's favourite mug with its picture of the Tolpuddle Martyrs. Harriet had

101

Googled Tolpuddle to check if it was on message. It wasn't of course, but a compromise had been reached whereby the offending mug was kept in a cupboard in the kitchen lest any visitor should get the impression that the ODA had been infected with socialism.

'Tea with three sugars, Minister.'

'Careful, Harriet. Walls have ears. You think you're keeping tabs on me. Well you aint a patch on Mrs. P. She's probably already got this place bugged to check I'm sticking to the diet. The sugar police are likely breaking the front door down as we speak. Anyoff, before they cart us away to the carrot juice club there's summat else I want to read. ODA port project at Tristan.'

'Maybe we should come to grips with world poverty before we start getting down to the finer details, Minister.'

He looked into her eyes and saw the spark of recognition flicker.

***

Sir Henry and Pike were in the Ambassador's office, Jardine propped on the edge of the desk and Pike, slightly stooped, shuffling and glancing about nervously in the middle of the carpet. Along the corridor the dinner party was still in full swing and Noriega's bragging monologue and occasional brayings from Mrs Reeves could still occasionally be heard even through the heavy oak door.

After a long pause made more ominous by the slow, reverberant ticking of a grandfather clock, Jardine looked across to Pike and smiled. Pike shuddered. It had been bad enough having to tell Sir Henry about the indiscretions of Prosperous Bay. It was even more embarrassing when Jardine had demanded to know *precisely* what had happened. Details that, not surprisingly, Pike had initially tried to gloss over. Details that Sir Henry seemed to relish.

But this was going to take the biscuit. Jardine was smiling and Jardine never smiled unless the roof was about to come in.

When he eventually spoke, Pike flinched.

'I suppose I could recommend you for the Victoria Cross for leading the invasion of Mrs Reeves and living to tell the tale. Hand to hand combat with a vastly superior force and all that. We fought them on the beaches. Didn't you, Mr Pike.'

'Wouldn't it be better if I just resigned, Sir?' Pike spoke so softly that a Noriega guffaw from the dining room almost drowned him out.

'Oh, no. Oh, most certainly, no. That would let you off the hook *altogether* too easily. More likely I'll suggest to London that you spend the rest of your miserable days filing ambassadorial expenses forms in some back office in Bermondsey. Or Baghdad. And if you even think of refusing, or, worse, if you try to take the coward's way out by resigning I'll tie you up in so many clauses of the Federation Official Secrets Act that you won't be able to waddle let alone cavort.' Jardine walked across to his drinks cupboard and poured a suicidal measure of malt. Pike almost allowed himself a sigh of relief. The emollient qualities of scotch on the Jardine temperament were well known. On the other hand, Sir Henry hadn't used the word 'bloody' in twenty minutes and that was a very sinister sign indeed.

When Jardine turned back from the drinks cupboard the smile had gone.

'But that's all something you can look forward to in the months to come. It's what we do in the meantime that's the problem. We can't be letting the love of your life go whispering about bloody harbours and container ships to dippy Donald during her pillow talk, can we?'

'They have separate rooms if that helps, Sir Henry.' Pike was clutching at straws.

'Oh, we have got our bare feet under the dressing table, haven't we?' Jardine cocked an eyebrow. 'But *do* they indeed. Must mention that one day at Joint Staffs.' He had a refill while he savoured the thought.

In a spirit of patriotism Pike hoped that the below stairs tittle tattle about Lady Ethne giving 'English lessons' to Momo hadn't travelled as far as the American embassy but wisely refrained from mentioning it.

'I could ask Lady Jardine to take her to one side and have a private word but once I've told her what the pair of you have been up to I think I know what that word would be.' Sir Henry feigned a shudder. 'Ethne can be harsh when faced with even a hint of common.'

For a micro second Pike considered gallantry but thought better of it.

'So it looks as if it's down to you, Mr Pike. It's the fifteenth today. Ignorance being Ambassador Reeves normal state of bliss it shouldn't be too difficult to keep him that way for a mere ten days. All you've got to do is allow your little liaison to blossom. Shouldn't be too much of a chore.' Jardine gave Pike a lecherous wink which was marginally more terrifying than the smile. 'Go swimming or whatever euphemism you choose, Mr Pike, as if your life depended on it. Which it probably does.'

***

Birtwistle scanned the shimmering horizon through his binoculars and thought that, despite the specimens it housed, this was probably the very nicest zoo in the whole world. The deep blue of the South Atlantic seemed to go on forever, sea merging seamlessly with sky. Below him, to the east, Bonfire Ridge fell away to a sun drenched Prosperous Bay Plain. He turned to look south over the island past Long Ground Ridge to Sandy Bay and then west past Mount Actaeon to the tumble of hills that ran out to Barren Ground. In the far distance was what had once been Blue Hill Village but was now being re-invented as Republika Srpska. Here and there he spotted flashes of wire topped border fence amongst the thick vegetation and out towards Stone Top to the south east the wooden towers of a frontier post stood proud of the trees. But apart from those tiny, distant fingerprints the place looked as if had been asleep for a thousand years.

He'd climbed out through eight feet high ferns and a forest of cabbage trees to Diana's Peak with the construction squad from Cable and Wireless who were installing a new radio relay mast. Wild canaries flittered in the vegetation as they passed. Hanrahan had come to supervise the works and while the riggers manhandled the dish into place on the gantry he asked to borrow Birtwistle's binoculars and map. He pointed out a summit called Halley's Mount that he'd read about in the Longwood library. 'Apparently it's where the great astronomer came in 1676 to record the transit of Venus. Unfortunately a passing cloud got in the way so he saw none of it. St Helena sods law.'

'There seems to be a lot of that about.'

A scarlet cardinal bird was a streak of vivid colour among the trees.

'And did you know?' said Hanrahan, positively twinkling with Longwood's fascinating facts.

'I'm sure I don't, but I'm equally sure you're going to tell me.'

'There were plans to bring Hitler here, if we'd managed to capture him alive of course. Keep him at Longwood. Churchill wanted to send him to the electric chair, of course – the gangster's penalty he called it, but others thought exile would get round the problems of how to give him a fair trial.'

'So not a lot of difference from Guantanamo, war on terror, all that stuff. But it must have sent a shiver through the French, the suggestion of putting Hitler in the same house where their great national hero had been banged up.'

'Not really. They were on our side by then.'

'I think I knew that.'

'Yes,' said Hanrahan, 'but it just goes to show you never really know who your friends might turn out to be.'

'As Tom Lehrer put it in one of his songs, talking about our current allies the Germans.' Birtwistle's tuneless baritone boomed out across Diana's Peak 'We beat them in 1918 and they've scarcely troubled us since then.'

Hanrahan smiled and turned the binoculars towards the north east coast and managed to identify the beaches of Prosperous Bay and Scraggy Point to the north of it. Beyond that was Turk's Cap Bay. Then he refocused and saw it. Most of it was tucked beneath the cliffs but just visible was a tiny square of gleaming white concrete surmounted by some sort of beacon. The nose of a mooring jetty.

'So what's really going on here?' Hanrahan asked Birtwistle when he handed back the binoculars.

'Sorry, no can do. Cable and Wireless will have to fill you in on the details – if indeed they know the details. But let's just say it's Military training. Guerrilla warfare, mountain and jungle, that sort of thing. Perfect place for it.'

And John F. Kennedy died of an in-growing toenail, thought Hanrahan.

'And you can't tell me about Liberia, Uganda and the Central African Republic, either I suppose, even though they keep cropping up on the email taps.'

'Fraid not. Except to say they're obviously potential trouble spots. Good idea to be prepared, know the lie of the land.'

And that's not the only lie, Hanrahan thought, but pushed his luck anyway. 'So Amin and Bokassa and the rest of the shady characters wandering about in Federation cyberspace are what? Code, a joke, a figment of somebody's imagination?' And then after a pause when they both looked out to sea. 'I know Duvalier's real enough because I've met him.'

"Sorry, not my department. You'd better check them out with personnel or look them up in the St. Helena telephone directory, which has to be the most interesting in the world if all the people you've been mentioning are real. And if they aren't ex directory.'

Hanrahan smiled his disarming broad smile and polished his spectacles.

'OK, so let's try safer ground. How's your security review going – or is that a figment of my imagination, too?"

"Oh, no. That's real as real can be. But it's fairly routine stuff as it turns out. Tweak here, tinker there is probably all it will amount to. That's the real security.' Birtwistle pointed out to sea. 'Twelve hundred miles of that stuff stops a lot of prying.' He looked at Hanrahan who held up his hands to show he'd got the message loud and clear and went back to supervising the alignment of the radio dish.

When he'd gone, Birtwistle took out the binoculars again and scanned Halley's Mount and then the section of coast to the north east that seemed to have taken Hanrahan's fancy. He was about to set off to walk down from the peak when he saw it, too. The tiny square of concrete with its navigation beacon, in shadow now but given away by the spray that broke from a running wave.

'Well, Mr Hanrahan,' he said under his breath 'obviously you're not the only one who's being kept in the dark.'

CHAPTER TEN

'I'm thinking of going, Alistair.'

'But has Dubya said you can?'

Tony Blair and his ever present mouthpiece were sitting in the gloom of the PM's office. The curtains were drawn and a single green shaded lamp on the desk gave the only light.

'No, I'm serious.'

'Tony, if you need a shit go have a shit. I don't give a shit.'

'Don't sulk Alistair. It's not attractive. And you know full well what I'm talking about – stepping down and leaving dear Gordon up to his sporran in the aforementioned.' Alistair Campbell allowed himself the faintest of smiles at the fragrant thought. 'But just because I've turned down a bit of advice is precisely no reason for you to be as offensive to me as you're paid to be to the press corps.'

'Well wash my mouth out with carbolic of mass destruction.'

'Talking of which, Alistair, we simply can't come clean the way you suggest. We're too far down the road for that.'

'We're not.'

'We are.'

'Not.'

'Are.'

Silence settled in the gloom for a few minutes. A quarter of a mile away Big Ben chimed nine.

'I can still make the lead on News at Ten.'

'No, Alistair, the transatlantic fall out would be horrible. Not to mention the hoo ha in Brussels and the UN.'

'It's going to be worse if you hold out for a fortnight and then spring it on them.'

'No, because by then it will be a fait accompli and there's precisely nothing they can do about it.'

'If you believe that, Tony, you've got you head so far up your arse that right now you must be looking at me through a set of teeth. But just before you cough and turn completely inside out, let me try one more time.'

The Prime Minister groaned and slumped back in his chair.

'We're talking virtual reality here, Tony. As that jerk press officer at the White House said before Iraq, we don't do discernible reality any more – the world doesn't work like that. So it's a game we're all playing by the same rules – them and us.'

'But which only works if we don't tell our respective electorates what the rules are.'

'Do me a favour. You know as well as I do they don't give an aforementioned so long as a six pack is less than a fiver and Ryanair will get you to Alicante for £9.99. Precisely 22% of them voted you in last time and half of them couldn't read English so they didn't know what the fuck they were voting for anyway.'

'Harsh, Alistair.'

'Harsh but democratically true. So bottom line, as Mr. Big Business next door would say, you could be David Icke reincarnated, getting advice from little green men on the Planet Zog, and they wouldn't know and they wouldn't care.'

'There's a considerable difference between little green men from outer space and a tried and trusted relationship with the President of the United States.'

Campbell let that pass and ploughed on.

'We've only got ten days left and you're already showing a passing resemblance to David Icke in this light so I'll get my advice in first before your head starts pulsing, your eyes come out on springs and the zogadoodles start speaking in tongues. Fact. We live in a shiny new land where we create our own reality. We did just that to justify getting rid of Saddam – you surely can't have forgotten so soon. Weapons of mass destruction, connections with 9/11, uranium bought from Niger to make a nuclear bomb. Greatest story ever sold. Happy days. All bollocks, as we know but it did the business. It let George and Tony, by appointment purveyors of democracy to the wide, wide world, march their men to the top of the

109

hill. Sure, you haven't yet worked out how to march them down again, but that's another reality we're running through the tweaking process as we speak…'

'All those things did was speed up the inevitable, as you well know, Alistair.'

'But it wasn't fucking true, Tony. I had to *make* it true.'

'And you did a great job, don't get me wrong, but this time's different because this time we're out on our own.'

'And as every schoolboy knows you should never let a politician out on his own. But lucky for you, Tony, I'm here with you in the valley of the shadow of deceit.' Campbell leaned forward and crossed his arms on the desk. 'Virtual reality will be our shield of righteousness and info-ganda our sword of truth. Hell, I sound like Jonathan Aitken – and there's a guy who missed his vocation.'

Blair got up and walked to the window, pulling back a curtain and looking down into Downing Street where a television crew was setting up its camera on the far pavement. 'However you dress it up we're pulling the wool over the eyes of our closest ally.'

'No, we're going to score a little PR victory, that's all.'

'And George won't like it.'

'OK, so this is going to be one occasion when he won't be able to dress up as Tom Cruise and ponce about on some aircraft carrier deck claiming he's saved the world, but even his own PR advisors are getting sick of that one, especially since the great victory that wasn't in Iraq.'

Blair let the curtain drop back into place and started to wander round the room.

'Look, Tony, this time we've got the drop on them for once.'

'But I don't see how we can come out of this business squeaky clean. Yes, America's using the Federation to get rid of some of its little diplomatic mistakes, but so are we. And arguably we're doing it for more devious reasons.'

'And by the time we've done the dance of the seven public relations veils round those they'll disappear like the conjuror's assistant.'

Blair had a momentary vision of a belly dancer with tinkling finger cymbals discarding veil after diaphanous veil. Unfortunately the dancer was Anne Widdicombe. It was a vision that would haunt him for some weeks.

'But more important,' Campbell continued, 'Guantanamo George is in deep doo doo with the international community. You are, too, of course but you come from a long line of what are seen as nasty, grasping imperialists, so all you've been doing is reverting to type. White man's burden and all that.'

Blair stopped in front of an ornately framed mirror and did lantern jaw practice.

'So?'

Jaw left. Jaw right. Jaw jutting proud.

'So are you listening, Tony because this is important.' The Prime Minister's jaw stopped clicking from side to side. 'So we've got to manage this news opportunity just as hard as we can. Anticipation, speculation, expectation, jubilation.'

'And how do we do that?'

'How we always do it. By leading the boys from the press by the dick until they get to the precise place we want them to be.'

'Which is?'

'God, you're slow today. Which is worshipping at the shrine of St. Tony of England.'

Blair looked back at the mirror and saw he was good.

'And if you really want to go, that same day we'll announce that in a spirit of humility and sacrifice you've decided to stand down – mission accomplished, time with Cherie (that'll take a bit of selling, he thought) other challenges, blah blah blah…'

'And?'

'And people who've been briefed till they bleed by the whips will beg you to stay. You won't of course, because you're going to get the legacy – Blair the patriot, Blair the brave, Blair the strong Prime Minister blah de blah. And even better than that the haggis basher gets to pick up the pieces. Sweet.'

Blair looked deep into the reflected eyes and said, 'Tell News

111

at Ten.'

Campbell didn't move. 'There is one Guy Gibson's dog in the woodpile, though, Tony.'

Blair, having made the decision, didn't want any hold ups on the road to canonisation. 'And what's that?'

'Prescott's still sniffing about. Harriet tells me he's been burying his bones in the Tinsley Shipping files. Turns out he knew Tinsley years back in Hull. Don't know if he's dug up anything about the special cargos but it might be wise to get him out of circulation for a bit.'

'Maybe George would have him in that CIA cage in Lincolnshire.'

'Appealing as that sounds it's a bit of an overreaction if I may say so. For all his obvious faults and even though he's got enough bulges to make him look like a passable suicide bomber, Presto's an unlikely Islamic terrorist. But he is Overseas Development Secretary so somewhere overseas would seem appropriate. And as he's so keen on islands in the South Atlantic we could make his day by sending him to one. Fact finding mission. I'll organise the facts.'

'Fix it,' said Blair, tidying away his papers into the red box. 'I thought you were going to ring News at Ten.' Campbell still didn't move but smiled at the Prime Minister across the desk.

'Bastard.' Blair slammed the box shut and yanked back the curtain again just in time to see ITN's dapper chief political correspondent slick his hair to perfection and pop his supercilious mug in front of the camera. 'Bastard. You already had.'

Campbell switched on the television as the virtual Big Ben bonged to the top of the hour and a fragrant virtual newsreader glided towards the camera.

'Saddam Hussein attacked what he described as the deceit of George Bush and Tony Blair at his trial in Baghdad today. The deposed Iraqi leader, looking markedly older than when he last appeared in court, made an impassioned attack on what he called western lies...'

Pictures of Saddam looking grey and drawn but angrily

shouting at court officials illustrated the story.

'Meanwhile in Afghanistan it's been reported that large numbers of UK forces have been deployed in the Margow Desert in western Helmand Province close to the border with Iran. This will be seen as a further attempt by the western powers to put pressure on President Mahmoud Ahmadinejad to abandon his nuclear ambitions. The deployment was immediately condemned by Iran and Syria as confrontational…'

Campbell switched off the set.

'Think you'd better ring the Chief of the General Staff and tell him what his troops are supposed to be doing. It might come as a bit of a surprise to him.'

CHAPTER ELEVEN

Ahna found Theo Bloor in the bar of the White Horse but this time there was no suggestion of a trip to paradise up the back stairs. Bloor belched as she slipped into the seat across the table and drained his glass. He'd been drinking since mid morning and could see two Ahnas with their overlapping smiles.

'Yuv sumn for me missa Bloor.'

'I had dear lady, but that was an opportunity shadly missed.'

Ahna looked at Bloor's belly resting on the table edge and thought that, amongst other horrors, something she'd missed was suffocation.

He fumbled in his waistcoat pocket and brought out a piece of crumpled paper which he pushed across the table while putting a finger to his lips.

'Shh..' Spittle appeared in the corners of his mouth.

Ahna put her hand on the paper and Bloor grabbed her wrist, leaning close to her face and breathing whisky fumes as he spoke. 'Not so fast my little tempress because I've got a message to company this piece of paper.' His elbow slipped off the table. 'You tell Mr Pineapple Face this is only part of what he wants to know.' He tapped the side of his head with an index finger which he then insinuated into the laces of her bodice and pulled her towards him. 'Tellm I don't give a shit about the pictures because what I've gots only vailable for money.' He was so close to Ahna's face now that she could have navigated by the road map of purple veins on his nose and cheeks. 'Letsay 50,000. You tell him, you hear. 50,000 pounds.'

Ahna pulled her head away, gathered up the paper and prised the finger from her dress. She stood and turned to go but then stopped and looked down at Bloor who was banging his glass on the table to get the barman's attention.

'I think you shouldv stuck to sex with lilgirls, Missa Bloo-er. Noso dangerous game.'

***

Hanrahan unfolded the piece of paper Florence Lacey had given him and smoothed it on the desk. As the night shift officer he had the silent Cable and Wireless control room to himself. He'd already sorted the evening's stack of communications into their respective file trays – three trays, jauntily labelled by some wag who'd done the job before him as BAD, MAD and DANGEROUS TO KNOW. There had only been a couple of BADs in that evening's batch – one of them an order from Amin to a company in the Ukraine for artillery pieces. Code Red. His request to a shop in Edinburgh for Scotland the Brave sheet music went into MAD. Depending on the sender, MAD requests were despatched to the quartermaster's department of the British or American Embassies and the orders would arrive some months later in the cargo of RMS St. Helena.

Bokassa's purchase order for a crate of homeopathic remedies and an imperial payment to the shopping cart of the London dealers Stanley Gibbons for an unperforated sheet of Penny Blacks were obviously MAD, too. But Charles Taylor's rambling letters to the Pope and the Archbishop of Canterbury about the evils of Gnosticism, particularly when used to underpin republican neo-con agendas went into DANGEROUS TO KNOW, the St. Helena equivalent of pending.

Some were more difficult to categorise; more subjectively problematical. An email from Aristide to George Bush using words the President couldn't possibly pronounce, let alone understand would, at first sight, belong in DANGEROUS TO KNOW. But a reference to the traditional Haitian custom of casting spells by making models of their victims and sticking pins in them, probably moved it up to MAD (Hanrahan recalled his conversation in the Longwood garden with Duvalier) while the attached list of US agents responsible for destabilising the Aristide regime gave it a further leg up into the BAD department. Code Red.

115

But most of the stuff that night was, as usual, just plain boring. Hanrahan had considered inaugurating a fourth file tray marked SILLY into which almost everything written by Pinochet or Noriega would go. Pinochet's constant complaints about communist spies in his hotel bathroom and Noriega's dry cleaning bills for his collection of military uniforms, which he insisted on sending directly to Mrs Reeves at the American Embassy, presumably because Panamanian dictators regarded laundry as womens' work.

Hanrahan switched on his laptop and studied the Florence Lacey paper. It was covered in a grid of letters and numbers which she'd suspected contained an access code to a file the Americans were keeping from their British partners on the Federation Joint Staff.

No big shakes, she'd said. She'd tried but couldn't crack it and anyway it would be a tad embarrassing if somebody on a computer in the British Embassy was found to be peek-a-booing into protected American codes. So would he be awfully sweet and so on and so on. Hanrahan spent two days rationalising the deceit.

He told himself it was just a bit of routine snooping; that the same cloak was being swished and the same dagger brandished in listening stations from GCHQ to the Hong Kong. In the end he settled for the fact it was an intriguing puzzle which would take the edge off the boredom. And also that it was payback for a spectacularly good shag on an Emperor's tomb. He cheered himself with the thought that not many third rate spies had been recruited in quite such exotic circumstances. Florence Lacey had been like a rabbit on steroids and when he eventually caught up with her he'd gasped 'Not tonight, Josephine' which had seemed like a good idea at the time but was a bit embarrassing in retrospect.

Hanrahan shrugged away the thought and logged on anonymously using one of the programmes that let C and W's monitors snoop about in the Colony's email accounts. For no better reason that having been bored out of his tree by the rant about Gnosticism he decided to work on Charles Taylor's Liberia platform. He typed in the grid of letters and numbers and ran the cryptography

programme that looked for patterns and linkages.
```
L 7 W 0 J 8 V S 6
Q R X I 2 P 3 N B
0 V B X H 9 F L Z
T 6 2 W J N X Q 4
Z 4 X R 5 P E N Y
G U H 4 M F 9 G U
A 2 C P V A C 6 M
```
The line of blue squares edged its way across the screen. After ten minutes he had a series of lists – names, dates, places, phrases, repetitions, anagrams and letter and number substitutions.

Of course this is where the real cryptographers earned their crust. To Hanrahan the lists were meaningless. There were a few names and places that jumped out at him – Mozart and Wordsworth, Sarajevo and Majorca. One or two dates chimed from school history lessons – the Battle of Trafalgar, the retreat from Moscow. For two hours he studied them until the letters and numbers began to blur into a crossword with a mind of its own but still he couldn't see any meaningful pattern.

He ran the programmes forward and back, algebraically and algorithmically. Nothing. But just as he was about to give up and spooling aimlessly through the lists he stopped at 'repetitions'. Among the options, F2 would delete duplicate letters and numbers. He hit it and the grid emptied dramatically, leaving just seven letters and four numbers.

I N S T Y L E 8 7 5 3

Hanrahan pushed his spectacles up onto his forehead and in five seconds flat realised he'd been trying to be too damned clever by half. It was as simple as ABC, or to be more precise T I N S L E Y –the shipping line and a file number. He accessed the System Restore Library which held backup copies of all the unmonitored files that routinely passed across the Federation Web. This was the tricky bit. Not leaving his electronic fingerprints. From the safe he brought the list of access codes which were automatically generated each day by the C and W mainframe and picked out the nine digit

code allocated that day to Donald Reeves.
Once into the system he typed in TINSLEY 8753. Invalid file. TINSLEY 7853. Invalid file. TINSLEY 3578. And up it came.
Confidential
Blout FCO
Ops Dir Tinsley Shipping
Ref Voyage 323
Additional to cargoes loaded Challenger at Tilbury as per previous manifest there will be one additional consignment to take aboard at (MAP REF TO ADD)
Rendezvous Ark Royal 20th 08.00. No radio traffic.
Consignment to be held secure area with 24 hour observation.
Assume this RV will allow sufficient time to make destination X2 on 25th 11 AM local time. Vital no slippage. Please confirm

'Well, damn me.' Said Hanrahan under his breath. It wasn't a file the Americans were keeping from the British. It was a message the British were keeping from everyone.

System Restore files couldn't be printed so Hanrahan wrote it out in longhand and put the paper in his pocket before logging off and ringing Florence Lacey to say they should meet. With luck there may be another spot of energetic vexillation tomorrow to disturb the Emperor's long sleep.

***

Pike wasn't enjoying his assignations with Dee Reeves anywhere near as much having been ordered to them by Sir Henry. The very thought of the Ambassador's smile had contraceptive qualities. There had been no repetition of the excitements of Prosperous Bay. They'd never been mentioned, even when on one of their swimming excursions Pike had raised the subject of the ship.

'Oh, by the way.' Casual as casual can be. 'That ship we saw up at the bay. Checked it out. Apparently some container ship on its way to the Cape with a spot of engine trouble. Lay in for shelter while they did the repairs.'

'Well that explains everything, Richard. Fancy another dip or would you preefer some tea?'

Five more days to go before he was off the hook. Five more days of tea and celibacy.

**

Donald Reeves, oblivious to the fact that he'd scarcely seen his wife for the best part of a week, was also counting the days. And in his bunker at the American Embassy as he counted he plotted. The map of the Colony laid out on the operations table was marked with troop deployments and routes of advance, strategic objectives and lines of supply.

Operation Just Deserts had been fought out in Reeves' head a dozen times and, so far, he'd always won. But the battle fatigue was beginning to show. He hadn't shaved for four days. His eyes were red rimmed for lack of sleep. Not that the Embassy staff could see any of this because Reeves had locked down for war. He wore a crumpled Lt. Colonel's uniform – the one that was normally pressed to perfection for American Ship Days. He ate battlefield rations. If he slept at all he slept on a camp bed beside the red telephone. He, at least, was prepared for the battle to come.

He'd retreated to the bunker after the call from Rumsfeld's office, the gist of which had been that the Colony had obviously sent Reeves stir crazy.

Between imaginary artillery bombardment and infantry advance Reeves re-ran the conversation.

'Mr. Secretary there's confirmed intelligence….'

'From where I'm sittin' that's not what I'm hearin'.'

'..Confirmed, 200% intelligence of a plan by A-min and Bo-kassa and

Taylor to….'

'Naaat again..'

'…stage a nuprisin' on the twenty fifth.'

'Now listen here, Reeves and you'll be able to listen better if ya stop rattlin' that desiccated walnut you call a brain inside that otherwise empty head a yours..' Rumsfeld had always prided himself

on his man management skills.
'So are ya listenin'?'
'Yessir.'
'ARE YA FUCKIN' LISTENIN'?'
'Yess Sir.'
'Well if yer listenin' it's worth me talkin'. That's the way the system works, right?'
'Right sir.'
'So, if yer listnin'. I don't want to trouble you with my problems. I won't even mention Ahmandinejad makin' nukes under his bed in I-ran. I'm not goin' to trouble you with Chavez setting' the world on fire in Venezuela. Don't bother yer pretty little face about the tea towel heads in Afghanistan and I-raq and Palestine. Never mind that Castro's wanderin' about in his pyjamas, ready to pop his little commie clogs and leave a power vacuum in Cuba. Hamas, Al Qaeda, Mujahiddin. I'll deal with them all, Mr Reeves. I'll handle it. All in a day's work.'
Suddenly, ominously quieter.
'But do me a little favour in return. Just one itsy bitsy favour, right?'
'Right sir.'
Full volume again.
'Don't bother me anymore with stories about some fuckin' sideshow starring three mad as racoons ex dictators who've got even smaller fuckin' walnuts than you.'
The long pause was filled with imaginary mortar fire.
'RIGHT?'
'Right.'
'And leave the thinking and the intelligence to me.'
The sound of the phone being slammed down crashed in Reeves' ear and momentarily drowned out the pdum pdum pdum of automatic weapons fire in his imagined battle.
The Ambassador turned to the operations table and put a finger on the toy tank parked in Jamestown Square. He drove it out onto Ladder Hill making throaty tank noises as is took the steep gradients.

'So somebody's bought Rumsfeld off, right? Right. So it's down to you cowboy, right? Right. And we're goin' to show him what doin' the job really means, right? Right. We're goin' to show him who's right, right? Right."
'Whumph.'
A tank round flew through Reeves' imagination deep into Liberia.
'RAH-ITE.'

***

The noise woke Charles Taylor in his bath. He opened one eye, snap and rotated it to the door. Tasawe was leaning against the frame tapping the stock of his Kalashnikov on the wall.

'How many times I gotta tell ya, boss. Coulda had ya fer dead if ahd a wanted to.'

The strategically placed towel laid across the bath to cover the Presidential private apartments exploded twice and bullets thudded into the wall, one on either side of Tasawe's head.

'And because I heard you on the stairs I could have had you dead twice over.' Taylor wiped off the pistol on the blackened towel. Tasawe smiled his black toothed smile but didn't mention that he hadn't come up the stairs.

'Boy's back from Bokassaland. Twenty guys max. is whole shootin'match he can getagether. So wid Amin's twentyfive an our thirty we don't zactly have sevent calvary.'

Taylor climbed out of the bath dripping onto the linoleum floor.

'It's enough, my man. He will pro-vide. He will walk with us through the paaaaths of righteousness.'

'It's the paaaths of glory ahm moren thinkin' bout, boss.'

Taylor started to sing as he towelled.

'My eyes have seen the glory….'

'And my eyes is seein' the marines and the tank.'

Taylor pulled the towel around his waist, walked across to Tasawe and gently held him by his shoulders.

'All we're going to do is teach them a little lesson, Tassie, a

121

little lesson in po-liteness.'

Tassie remembered some of Taylor's po-lite little lessons from the past and the po-lite, tidy little heaps of bodies that were usually left afterwards, but didn't mention them.

'He works in mysterious ways, my man.'

And so do you. Another Tasawe thought that didn't see the light of a bright Liberian day.

***

Lady Jardine's English lessons with Momo had again reached the letter F. She was a good teacher and he had been a quick learner. Past imperfect to present tense in about eight weeks. But today, rather more tense than usual because they were in the Embassy annex and Sir Henry was just two floors away in his office. The annex was where Lady Jardine played host to her various groups of ex pat ladies – yoga for beginners and line dancing, the Federation branch of Pilates for health and power aerobics. None of them as strenuous as English lessons.

'Momo?'

Momo was lying on the floor looking for all the world as if he'd been set upon by the Bulgarian women's championship line dancing team. Ethne Jardine ran her hand over his gleaming chest.

'Momo, you're most awfully kind, you know that, don't you?'

He still hadn't got his breath back sufficiently to reply.

'So….I just know you'll be happy to do me a little service – another little service.' She smiled down at him and her grey eyes twinkled. "I think it's time you had a few days off to go travelling and I thought Uganda and the Central African Republic would be nice at this time of year. She slithered into her pink twin set. 'Travel does so broaden the mind and it's quite amazing what little tid bits one can pick up from the locals.'

It being Momo's afternoon off he slipped into shorts and sweat shirt and Ethne reached up and gave him a chaste peck on the cheek.

'And I'll so look forward to de-briefing you when you get back.'

***

'And I'll so look forward to de-briefing you when you get back...'

Sir Henry smiled into the ripples in his whisky glass and switched the receiver in his desk drawer from the bug to the BBC World Service.

As ever Ethne had been a star and she had such a bloody marvellous way of mixing business with pleasure.

The BBC newsreader, who was almost as breathless as Momo had been a few minutes before was reporting on the meeting of the UN Security Council in New York.

'President Ahmadinejad of Iran refused to back down about his uranium enrichment programme and accused the western powers of using bullying tactics, singling out Britain for particular criticism following its deployment of troops along the eastern Iranian border. Meanwhile, there was further criticism of the United States from the Venezuelan leader, Hugo Chavez. He described President Bush as 'the devil' and said he knew he'd been there the day before because there was still a smell of sulphur in the room....'

Sir Henry thought he'd use that one on Reeves, if ever the devil's disciple emerged from his bunker.

'Other world news. There's speculation at Westminster that Tony Blair is planning to stand down as Prime Minister before the next election. Gordon Brown, the Chancellor of the Exchequer is the clear favourite to replace him. And there are unconfirmed reports from Saudi Arabia that one of the leaders of Al Qaeda has died of typhoid in his hideout in the mountains between Pakistan and Afghanistan...'

'Two dangerous buggers gone in one day, then.' Sir Henry switched off the radio and settled down for his afternoon nap.

But it was a fitful sleep, troubled by dreams. He and Ethne were dressed in Victorian finery in a box at the Hammersmith Empire watching a pantomime by gaslight. Tony Blair and George Bush were the ugly sisters. Pike was Buttons and Mrs Reeves a pulchritudinous Cinderella. The pit orchestra wound its rendering of the Zimbabwean national anthem to a wavering crescendo and Donald Reeves entered stage right as Prince Charming. Part Elvis Presley, part Liberace, he shimmered with sequins as he marched to the front of the stage brandishing a crystal slipper. But instead of presenting it to Cinderella he raised it high above his head as he went down on one knee and looked directly at Ethne. As Henry turned to look at her she trilled 'Some day my prince will come….' There was a flash and a mushroom cloud of smoke and Ethne the Fairy Godmother flew down and took Reeves' hand and the pair of them soared away past the dress circle and disappeared, twinkling into the darkness. When Henry looked back to where Ethne had been he found Idi Amin dressed as principal boy and wheezing his bagpipes into life. As he played 'Donald Where's Yer Troosers' the Foreign Secretary beamed insincerity and led the company forward to a curtain call.

'Henry….'

'Hen-ry….'

When Ethne managed to shake him awake he was sweating slightly and said, 'Reeves has flown away covered in sequins…'

'It was only a matter of time, Henry. But another piece of good news. Momo's agreed to do a spot of undercover work.'

And Henry went back to sleep smiling and had happier, more vigorous dreams.

CHAPTER TWELVE

The passenger terminal at RAF Brize Norton was asleep. A few groups of Squaddies dozed in corners, using their kit bags as pillows. Sandwiches curled lazily on the coffee bar counter. Even the one armed bandits were flashing more lethargically that their brothers in the real world. Irish pubs, duty free shops and book stores selling chick lit novels and self improvement manuals were there none. The overhead display screens announced departures to destinations that hadn't yet made it onto the Easyjet map – Kandahar and Ascension Island and Basra, but as a rowing boat was to the QE2 so Brize Norton was to Heathrow.

Then an automatic glass door shuddered open and the Squaddies and curling sandwiches were rudely awakened by a voice that echoed round the emptiness.

'Nearer my God to thee. It's like a bloody undertaker's waiting room.'

Prescott bounced into the lounge, Mr Blobby on holiday, while Harriet, his minder, struggled with two suitcases and a red box. The Deputy PM and Minister for Overseas Development was travelling incognito and doing it very well. The sunglasses and sandals were good, but the luminescent Caribbean shirt and creased Bermudas were nothing short of genius. Below the shorts emerged legs of such a deathly pallor that the DPM's analysis of the place could have been right and he could have been a client.

The RAF check in clerk looked him up and down with undisguised distaste as Harriet manhandled the cases onto the baggage conveyor. Prescott pushed his diplomatic passport across the desk with a look that could have stripped paint. The clerk glanced down at the details in the passport then back to the embodiment of Viva Espagna standing in front of him. The world being an essentially unfair place it was the clerk who blushed. 'Sorry, Deputy

Prime Minister, didn't recognise you for a minute for some reason. I'll get someone to take you to the quiet lounge right away.'

Prescott took off the sunglasses and looked around the room which had settled back into siesta time. He wondered how any lounge could possibly be quieter. 'The Ascension flight's on time, sir. Take off in about an hour.'

'When you say quiet you mean first class?'

'Fraid there's no first class on the Tri Star services, sir,' said the clerk. Then in an attempt to redeem himself. 'Very egalitarian, the armed services.'

The Prescott jowls trembled. 'Which like as not explains why you can't move for Brigadiers and Lt. Colonels. Knee deep in the buggers.' Then leaning towards the clerk who slid as far back into his chair as it was possible to be without disappearing into the upholstery. 'And 'egalitarian' is a *frightfully, frightfully* big word for common as muck working class lads like you and me.'

Harriet coughed. 'Perhaps the quiet lounge would be a good idea and I can give you a bit of background.'

As Prescott walked past the heap of dozing soldiers he gave them a quick chorus of Una Paloma Blanca at peak volume. Two of the soldiers fell off their kitbags and another sprang to attention shouting 'Yes, Serg' before his eyes were open.

Sort of person that gets the working classes a bad name, the clerk thought as the door of the quiet lounge closed behind the Minister for Tuneless Singing.

Harriet opened her briefcase and took out the DPM's itinerary. 'So, then. Eight hours or so down to Ascension then we'll probably have to stay overnight to wait for the Tinsley Challenger. She's expected in tomorrow but could arrive earlier. Then three days at sea down to St Helena where we'll be staying at the Embassy. Busy schedule, I'm afraid. New school to officially open. Actually it's been open for six years but you're the first Minister to get down there for ages so we're mopping up a bit. Then there's a tour of the Cable and Wireless monitoring station and a plaque to unveil on some new radio mast or other.'

'Is this your idea of a holiday? It sounds about as much fun as caravanning with Margaret Beckett.'

'There's more, Minister. Lots of jolly activities because it can be soo boring just lying on the beach all day, don't you find? So the island flax company has organised a little seminar you're going to chair. They want us to send a ship to take the crop off the island every year but we can't do that for obvious reasons (they were anything but obvious to Prescott) so you just have to keep shaking hands and telling them you'll organise a full cost benefit analysis the moment you get back. That should keep it on the back burner for at least ten years.'

'Then a spot of snorkelling? Horse riding through the surf? Croquet with a gin sling in one hand and a dusky maiden in the other?'

'Don't think Mrs P would approve, Minister.'

'No, she's never been keen on snorkelling. Messes up her hair.'

'There will be the usual round of drinks parties, glad hand the Americans and the French, that sort of thing, which I'm sure you'll be very good at. But I would advise you to go easy on the jokes, Minister. They can so easily misfire when addressed to people with no known sense of humour like the Americans and the French.'

'There was this black man who went into a bar with a parrot on his shoulder and the barman said 'where did you get him?' And the parrot said 'Africa. There's thousands of them over there.'

'Quite. But there's one final engagement. British Council. They've got some artist or other – Bloor I think he's called - who's on the island to create a conceptual artwork which captures its ethnographic diversity. Not quite sure what that means but I'm sure you won't need to know what it means to unveil it. All you have to do is pretend you like it and whip off the old sheet.'

'I think you're talking grannies and eggs here. MPs are taught how to unveil before they're taught how to read.'

No sign of surprise appeared on Harriet's face.

'War memorials, Princess Dianas, plaques on factory walls.

Done 'em all. But this modern arty farty stuff problem is you can't tell which is the art and which is the artist. Once met Gilbert and George. Had to unveil George on a plinth in Trafalgar Square but I think I unveiled Gilbert because George had piles. Or maybe I'm mixing up two unveilings.'

'Rule of thumb, Minister. If it farts and shakes hands it's probably the artist. If it looks like an unmade double bed in which somebody has farted it's probably the art. And it if it looks like an unmade bed *and* farts it's probably Michael Foot re-incarnated.'

Prescott gave a volcanic chuckle.

'You know, lass, I was determined not to like you but I think working with Prescott's gonna be the makin' of you.'

***

There had been times during his posting to the Colony when Momo had wished he'd stayed in Brixton but this wasn't one of them. It was a spectacularly beautiful morning. He'd climbed out of the valley mist and was walking along a high, undulating, Wizard of Oz sort of road just over the Ugandan border. The verges were lined with thickets of Kaffir thorn and occasional, startling clumps of hibiscus. The breeze made a groaning noise in the waving fields of flax that stretched away on either side. Momo had sat down to check where he was and to drink from a metal cistern of cool, clear water by the roadside. A wizened old Saint leading a dusty train of pack donkeys stopped and chatted for a while and introduced himself as Solomon and told Momo he was at a place called Half Tree Hollow but he couldn't remember why it was called that and he couldn't point it out on the map.

Perhaps a mile further on Momo first heard the banshee. At first he thought the noises were just tricks of the wind in the line of eucalyptus and pine that had drawn in on the road. But they were getting louder. The screams and wheezing gasps of a creature in agony seemed to rise out of the fields, first on one side, then the other and as they rose they hung in the humid air.

Then round a corner in the road, narrowed by tall clumps of

encroaching prickly pear, he saw it and heard it in all its horror. A kilted and sporraned black piper, strutting and prancing, led a rag tag line of men in Oxfam shop uniforms. Occasionally the leader would take his mouth from the squawking pipe and shout a command. 'Leffnrightnrightnleff'. The soldiers behind him did a little dance of incompetence and went back to the left, stumble, right, right, stumble, left they were doing before. Twenty five soldiers and twenty six parades.

'Bydright. HALT.'

They clattered to a standstill, several of the squad walking into the man in front. The piper squeezed the bag to strangled extinction and turned to face the motley squad behind him. Field Marshal cum Sergeant Major, Amin berated them for some minutes. The character and usefulness of their mothers, wives, vital organs and sexual paraphernalia were all called into question in a rant that roared up from his scuffing boots. He was leaning so close to the nearest soldier that one of the bagpipe drones threatened to disappear up the man's left nostril.

'An' meezuntinkin' less you square up sharpish fellas you been gonna end up croc chow pronto time. Cept yo stupid heads goin' in freezer fo me play chess game wid later....'

'Sweet,' thought Momo, trying to pretend he was a prickly pear.

''N whez yo uniform? You awol fella? Deeserter mebbe....?'

Momo realised he was talking to him as the great head swivelled and the yellowed eyes looked him up and down.

' N you know what happnin' deserted fellas, mister...' Amin clicked his tongue and mimed a head ricked to one side in a noose.

'Nossir. I's just on holiday, just passin' through..'

'Just passin' away, mo like mister ifn you don be fallin' in pronto time ya listenin'..?'

One of the soldiers giggled. Amin's arm shot out and a vast hand grabbed the offender by the collar, lifted him off his feet and pulled him out of the line.

' N you gonna be soldierburger fore you can shit yoself mister.' He dropped the soldier and waved Momo into the line 'FALL DE

129

HELL IN.'

Briefly Momo wondered if he should mention his job at the Embassy, his time in the Royal Marines, that his mother loved him, but decided on all counts that this probably wasn't the moment. He shrugged, picked up his rucksack and marched into line, coming smartly to attention and crisply saluting his new and hopefully only temporary commanding officer.

'Sah.'

'You bin done this someplace else Ibintinkin. Mebbe you getting promoted garrson sergt major knock dis rabble into shape Itinkin. Fore I disarm em.'

Amin's face broke into a wide grin.

'An' disleg dem. An' dishead dem.'

He chuckled at his little joke and clapped his hands and his audience laughed along with him.

Momo, too, opted for self preservation. He spun round to the lounging squad, stamped first one foot then the other and shouted in the clipped cockney accent favoured by all parade ground sergeants from wherever they happen to come. 'You 'orrible little men. You'se gonna wish you 'adn't been born..' He marched along the line, adjusting tatty uniforms and rusty guns as he went. 'Lee-eft tun.' He pointed to give them a clue. Amin fired up the pipes, launched into what may possibly have been Flowers of the Forest and the pride of the Ugandan army marched away to barracks.

***

Back in Jamestown it was rather more tuneful in the lounge of the Consulate Hotel. President Aristide, still failing in his attempts to get through to George Bush, had taken to passing the time by playing the grand piano in the palm court each afternoon. His selections from Gilbert and Sullivan blended well with the faded Edwardian surroundings but Iolanthe and The Pirates of Penzance seemed strangely at odds with his audience. Sullivan's *Pineapple Poll* might have been more appropriate given that Manuel Noriega was in a far corner in animated conversation with Ahna. He jabbed a finger at the piece of crumpled paper and banged a fist on the starched table cloth, dislodging an apple tart from the tiered cake stand.

At a table nearer the piano two colourfully dressed gentlemen drank strong coffee and swapped stories about treacherous America. One of them, the very model of a modern major general, or to be more precise brigadier general, wore golden epaulettes on a uniform of midnight blue and a sash crafted from what any passing vexillologist would immediately recognise as the Paraguayan flag.

'Such big a fuss over such little a man.' Alfredo Stroessner Matiauda, who looked like an ageing cherub, shook his head. For some minutes, as the music changed to *Two Little Maids From School*, they'd been chatting about Josef Mengele, the Nazi prison camp doctor that Stoessner had resolutely refused to extradite to Israel and the 200,000 other friendly Nazis who'd found refuge in Paraquay during the thirty odd years Stroessner was President.

'So who cares? We took them because they were good soldaten; strong German stock like me fighting the long and lonely war against the kommunistisch. Until Carter and Reagan ratted on the deal and threw me to the red wolves. Me, who had been their staunchest ally in times of trouble.'

'At least Reagan didn't try to blow you to bits.' The second man spoke in a strangely sing-song voice and smiled and the heavy bags under his eyes rose and fell. 'But that was in the bad old, naughty old days.' He tutted quietly and waggled his finger. 'Your mistake, Alfredo, is you haven't spotted the benefits of being a reformed character. Like me.' He threw his arms wide.

The 'me' in question was swathed in a robe of many colours and had tight curled hair bursting from under a small round hat that gave him a passing resemblance to Chico Marx. But none of the Marx brothers, even in their wilder flights of fancy, ever had a title so grand – Guide of the First of September Great Revolution of the Socialist People's Libyan Arab Jamahiriya, Brotherly Leader and Guide of the Revolution – Muammar Abu Minyar al-Gadaffi for short.

'You got 'socialist' in your title my friend. So you deserve to be blown to kingdom come.' In the Stroessner years the President had been renowned for his skill at making people disappear. Now you see them, now you don't see them ever again.

'Oh, our kingdom come before you know it, Mr once upon a time. Islamic States of Europe first. Ten years, no more. We're breeding like Arabs and we got lotsa wives. Might take a bit longer in a primitive place like Paraguay....'

They gently squabbled on like handsomely plumed cockerels in a hen run.

The Mugabe children were playing a noisy game of hide and seek in a clump of potted palms close to hotel reception, while the recently arrived Zimbabwean President and his wife made small talk with a man who'd been their house guest in Harare for some years. Small world.

The two men were comparing moustaches. Robert Mugabe was saying it should have been perfectly obvious he'd copied his moustache from Charlie Chaplin not from Hitler. He gave a Great Dictator straight armed salute. They all laughed and the children copied him. Grace Mugabe offered more tea and pulled a face as Aristide launched into *A Wandering Minstrel I*. The other man at the Mugabe table stroked his own, rather more luxuriant moustache and said he was very definitely an Emiliano Zapata man, himself.

'Better – to – die – on – your – feet – than – live – on – your - knees.' He proclaimed, enunciating each word as if it was a stranger to him.

'But those were the days when heroes of the revolution got the respect they deserved," Mugabe added urbanely, his little moustache doing a jig on his lip.

'Except Zapata was assassinated by the Mexican army if I'm not much mistaken.' Said Grace. 'Doesn't sound very heroic or respectful to me.'

'One – of – the – hazards – of – the – job.' Mengistu Haile Mariam, murderer of Emperor Haile Selassie and Head of State in Ethiopia for a spell, knew all about the hazards of the job. It had

132

been the old 'didn't kill enough of his enemies while he had the chance' hazard that had seen him deposed to the Mugabe's spare bedroom.

As the piano tinkled on, the old men swapped their grumbles about the various world leaders who'd hung them out to dry – Blair pulling the plug on Mugabe; Gorbachev being a wimp in Russia and cutting off Mengistu's arms supply; Nelson Mandela cosying up to the imperialists; George Bush Senior backing regime change in Ethiopia.

'And now illegal regime change runs in the family. And they have the nerve to accuse us of illegality.' Said Mugabe with statesmanlike distaste.

Grace, who since her arrival in the Colony had re-branded herself as Earth Mother, added more water to the pot and said 'Oh, but it could have been so much worse, Robert. You've really got to learn to look on the bright side. They've given us a bit of pretend Zimbabwe – so much easier to run than the real thing. No affairs of State, no inflation, no banned opposition parties sneaking about.' Her background in secretarial dictation had instilled a streak of practicality in Mrs Mugabe. 'And people aren't forever criticising you here and journalists aren't trying to creep across the border to cause trouble. And, best of all, we've avoided ending up against a wall like the Ceaucescus.' Spoken with a flourish.

'Grace.' Sharply, in a 'master in his own house' sort of tone. 'I've told you many times that the C word is unwelcome. Even to mention it suggests we could be in the same league as those awful people.'

'And – what – sort – of - leader,' said Mengistu airily, 'makes – speeches – to – crowds – that - haven't – had – the – bad – elements – weeded - out.' Remembering the image that went round the world of a little, black-hatted, faltering Ceaucescu on a balcony being heckled into silence. 'Even – Tony – Blair – slings – hecklers – out – of – his – party - conference.' The once leader of Ethiopia had apparently overlooked the fact he'd escaped from the country by the skin of his teeth and that most of his supporters had, indeed, ended up against a pock marked wall.

'And what sort of leader hasn't already locked up the family of the chap who's going to fly his escape helicopter,' said Mugabe, dismissively, remembering that the Ceaucescus had been handed over to the opposition by their pilot.

'The only point I'm making, as you know Robert, and I'm sure it applies to you, too..' Grace turned her matriarchal smile on Mengistu. '..is that strong and talented leaders show strength and talent to the end, even when the tides of ingratitude begin to run.'

It was at that point, midway through a boisterous rendering of *Strephon's a Member of Parliament,* that the music suddenly stopped. Conversations round the room slowly died away and the Mugabe children abandoned the potted palms and ran back to hide behind their mother's chair. A leaden silence broken only by the occasional nervous cough fell on the palm court of the Consulate Hotel.

Aristide was on his feet by the piano, staring at the tall, lumpy man with sideburns who stood just inside the door with a pretty young Saint on his arm.

'Heard you was in town,' the man by the door said as he started to stroll with his companion towards the pianist. 'And as it's Napoleon Day the French are all lying drunk in a corner singing the Marseillaise so I thought I'd take the chance to see the sights..' he glanced down at the girl and back to Aristide '..and I thought maybe we could both catch up on the news from home. Call this visit a postcard from Haiti.'

Aristide was mouthing like a fairground goldfish and clenching and unclenching a fist by his side. When he spoke his voice caught in his throat.

'I don't...I don't tittle tattle with thugs and murderers, Mr Duvalier.'

The Saint girl started to look a touch nervous but still clung to Duvalier's arm.

'Well you sure must have had a lot of lonely, quiet days in Haiti. Couldn't even have a cosy 'tittle tattle' with yourself if even half the stories I hear is true.'

'That's a lie put about by the Americans to justify their illegal actions, as you well know.' Aristide was shouting and for a moment so looked as if he was going to lash out that the Saint girl flinched.

'Yo…' Duvalier held up the palms of his hands and summoned a dose of emollient insincerity '..we don't have to *like* each another; we don't have to send each other Christmas cards; you don't have to let your daughter marry one…' The Saint, who was certainly young enough to be Duvalier's daughter, extricated her arm and sidled away to a safe distance. '…But you got to admit we do have a few things in common. One ex President to another and both shafted by the Washington witch doctors, who make voodoo look like hymn singing.'

In their corner Mugabe and Mengistu nodded silent agreement.

'So what's the problem having a little chat about where Haiti goes from here?'

But it was probably going to be a fairly one sided little chat because Aristide had temporarily lost the power of speech.

Mengistu leaned across to Mugabe and said 'I – suppose – stranger – things – have - happened.'

***

John Prescott hadn't slept well. He'd been woken several times by the roar of ageing tri-star jets lumbering along the runway just a few yards from his bedroom window. He was in Bunk Bed City, the huddle of huts that provide transit accommodation on the perimeter of the appropriately named Wideawake Airfield on Ascension Island. The Tinsley Challenger had been delayed and was due off Georgetown at breakfast time.

He rolled out of the ruck of bedclothes and switched on the TV. BBC World was reporting on the comments of the Chief of the General Staff that the British army was doing more harm than good in Iraq and that Afghanistan was the place to be.

'They're starting to come out of the woodwork,' Prescott said to himself as he started to shave. He almost took an ear off when the

135

Prime Minister's spokesman popped up to say there wasn't a cigarette paper between the General's views and Tony Blair's. 'Bollocks.' He dabbed his grazed cheek.

Campbell was in full flow. 'When the Prime Minster says we have to stay for as long as it takes and the General says we have to leave Iraq soon to avoid breaking the army, they're saying exactly the same thing. If there's a debate at all it's simply about the finer points of timing.' Campbell repeated the same line several times no matter what question his increasingly frustrated interviewer asked. It was his usual technique. Say something often enough and it becomes the truth.

'And people accuse me of mangling the English language,' said Prescott as he started to climb into an even more garish outfit that the one which had enlivened Brize Norton the day before.

The life jackets were dowdy by comparison when, an hour later, Prescott and Harriet were in the Georgetown lighter, pitching and rolling past the moored tanker that provided fuel for the airbase and heading towards the unmarked ship on the eastern horizon. Harriet was trying to take her mind off the motion by explaining the incontrovertible truths enshrined in everything Campbell had said. She must have been up half the night being briefed by Downing Street, thought Prescott. Maybe explains why she's looking so green. Downing Street briefings had a similar effect on him.

They came alongside a wall of grey steel streaked with rust which towered over them and a slim companionway snaked up to the rail. The lighter rose and fell past the platform on which four crewmen waited to catch the passengers and bring them aboard. One minute ten feet below, the next ten feet above. The lighter's engines raced to keep it as close as possible to the container ship and the next time its deck rose to approach the platform Harriet was told to jump. Two of the crewmen caught her by the arms and hoiked her aboard. Two or three swells later they tackled the rather weightier challenge of getting eighteen stone of Government Minister onto the ladder. Prescott jumped and four sets of hands held tight, but an elegant embarkation it was not. The cases and red box followed, the lighter swung away to Georgetown and the tone of the ship's engines deepened as it headed south.

'Must organise an early day motion against live animal exports when I get back,' said Prescott to one of the bemused crewmen who was delicately checking his incipient hernia. At the top of the long climb the tall figure of Harry Tinsley stood at the gap in the rail.

'Bugger me, another chance missed. I could have got a life peerage like as not if you'd gone in the drink.' He held out one of his fingered spades and shook Prescott's hand. 'From the Labour Party, of course. The Tories'd never forgive me for losing their best asset.'

Harriet, still swaying slightly, stored the greeting away for use one afternoon in the Commons tea room as a steward showed her to her cabin.

After she'd gone to be sick Prescott said, 'Nay, Harry, surely yer old mate's worth more than 150,000 measly quid and that's all you need for a gong. The buggers'll take green shield stamps and co-op milk tokens if you approach them right. You want to be Lord Tinsley of whadjemecallit, just say the word.'

'Word is, maybe you can't swing things the way you used to. And that's because somebody's got your tackle in the mangle.'

'Now am I talking with a high squeaky voice, Harry? Do I look like somebody as been emasculimated?'

'You look like nowt on earth if you want the truth," said Harry looking at the palm trees on the shirt and his reflection in the sporty sunglasses.

'Under cover, Harry. Embedded..'

'We're either talking Hazel Lewthwaite again or you've been on the sauce.'

'At least I've got here. And you didn't think I'd get this far. Go on, did you?'

'Mebbe you're right at that. But you did once get lost going from home to school – and that was when you were 43 and going in a Ministerial car to open the new science block.'

'Aye but this time I were cannier, if I say so myself. Chauffeurs get lost, particular if they're Jimmy Lightfoot. And I only employed

137

him because his dad once got me out of a spot of bother with the hooker of Holland when we were on the ferries. Anyoff, that's best forgotten. What I'm saying is Civil servants from the Department of Overseas Missionary Work, don't get lost. They could get you to Ulan Bator with their eyes shut. And before you say owt, no I don't know where it is, except it's the capital of Monrovia.' He paused to allow the self effacing erudition to sink in. 'But they do get baffled. Little hooray Harriet there knows I'm up to summat but she can't for the life of her work out what. And all I've got to do is keep her guessing for another few days and, bingo, I can settle back and do me memoirs.'

'Oh, and they'll be a joy to read. From where I remember you used to struggle writing betting slips.'

'Nay, I'd get one of them ghastly writers to do them. Anyoff, I'm only *threatening* to write them. After Blunkett wrote his and blew the gaff on all those little Cabinet disagreements, just the mention of memoirs sends Tony screaming to the lavvy.'

Harry Tinsley couldn't help but smile at the thought of the Prime Minister racing down the corridor with his trousers round his ankles and a guide dog in hot pursuit. 'Aye, but to be able to bring on a fit of the skitters you've got to get home first and most people who take this run have a one way ticket.'

'H-a-r-r-y.' In a 'how can you be so stupid' sort of tone. 'I've got back alive from Party Conferences in Bournemouth. And that was the days when the Labour Party was stabbing itself in the front.'

Harry shrugged. 'Your business. But my business…' he looked forward to the open sea past the containers stacked on the deck '… my business is to take you one way and leave you there. So I'd better get you settled in, shipmate.' He ducked through a door into a white painted corridor lit by fluorescent tubes and Prescott trailed along behind. 'You'll need to get your bearings 'cause it's a maze in here. This is deck five. You and yer minder are one up on six and above that is the bridge deck. We've an open bridge policy. Go up and look at the charts, have a crack with the duty officers if you want. If they're doing anything tricky they'll tell you to bugger off.' He started up a companionway ladder. 'The one spot that's out of bounds...' Harry stopped half way up and turned to Prescott. '...And I mean one hundred percent off limits, even to James Bond's fat uncle, is deck four. High security deck. Armed guards who'll shoot your knackers off soon as look at you. Understand?'

Prescott crossed his hands on his crotch and smiled sweetly. 'Well, shiver me timbers.'

***

At the same moment, eight hundred miles to the south, Sir Henry Jardine was enjoying that most enervating of blood sports - Foreign Secretary baiting, or pig sticking as it was known colloquially when one or two Ambassadors were gathered together in the bottom of a glass.

'Well, since you ask, Foreign Secretary, personally, I could disagree with very little of what the Chief of the General Staff had to say. We're obviously making a proper bloody goulash of Iraq....' The Ambassador was settled in his office chair with his feet on the desk. The red telephone was tucked between cheek and shoulder and he was studying his carefully manicured fingernails.

'Sir Henry, I'll make sure Her Majesty's First Minister has the benefit of your expert advice at the very earliest opportunity, but...'

'About time somebody gave our esteemed PM some advice that was worth listening to, F Sec. Make a change from him having his head patted and nappies changed by Nanny Bush.' The line from London was, momentarily, silent. 'Still there, Foreign Secretary?' Henry asked mischievously. A cough came down the line. 'Oh, good, thought you might have popped down to Chequers to report on dissention in the ranks..' He smiled across at Ethne.

'As you well know, Sir Henry, dissention is discouraged by the present administration, quite simply and sensibly because it stands in the way of good governance. And if I may be permitted to say so you're straying rather close to the bounds of unacceptability...'

'Ah...Acceptability.' He said the word slowly and emphatically and it brought another silence during which, Henry imagined, the

Foreign Secretary was remembering youthful indiscretions in general and a certain lively party at which they'd both been present at the Embassy in Riga, in particular.

'Quite, Sir Henry. But I think we should concentrate on more pressing matters.'

'And as we know, Foreign Secretary, there is nothing in the world more pressing than covering one's own back.' Ethne mimed thrusting a dagger into her breast as she swept Sir Henry's glass from the desk and set off across the room to get him a refill.

'The pressing matters to which I refer have rather more to do with Affairs of State.' Pompous bloody ass, thought Henry. 'Matters of timing and personnel and security planning.' The Foreign Secretary began to rattle off the details before Sir Henry could interrupt again. 'Both the Bellerophon and the Tinsley Challenger are on schedule. They'll arrive with you on the 25th as planned. It's important that you meet the Challenger at Turk's Cap..'

'One little maggot in the marmalade. That's going to mean having an American Ship Day in Jamestown and Reeves is still locked up tight in his bunker biting the heads off Taliban guerrillas..'

'We're aware of that particular problem and the PM has talked to Rumsfeld. Not given him all the details, of course, but suggested that because of the fall out from the Joint Staffs dispute, whereas it would obviously be inflammatory for you to take over an American Ship Day, we could offer a diplomatic half way house by making it a more, how shall I put it…. ceremonial occasion and having the Keeper of the Regalia officiate because she of course works for both administrations. Infringes several chapters of Atlantic Rules, of course. Wouldn't stand up in any meaningful international forum but I'm sure you'd agree that Ambassador Reeves' head scarcely falls into that category.'

'I think we just found a subject on which we can agree whole heartedly, Foreign Secretary.'

'And it's *so* satisfying when diplomatic negotiations reach a successfully accommodation, don't you think?' The patrician sneer had edged back into his voice. 'But there is one other rather sticky

140

little matter that you should have cognisance of, Ambassador..' Yes, never use a simple word when a bloody complicated one will do, thought Henry. '…Because of matters beyond our immediate control…' As so many things were, Henry thought. '..Bellerophon will be arriving with not one but two passengers.'

'Well I hope they're on speaking terms because it's a very small quay and we have a very small honour guard who wouldn't know the difference between a rifle and an entrenching tool and I'm not sure how Miss Lacey's going to cope if they wander off the bloody ship and start knocking seven bells out of each other.'

'Unlikely. Totally different spheres of interest. Nothing to worry about on that score.'

He gave Sir Henry two names and then a third which curdled Sir Henry's afternoon. When, some minutes later, the Ambassador slowly put the phone down he said to Ethne, who'd propped herself on his chair arm, 'Well, no wonder everybody's so bloody touchy. Seems the Americans are on the fiddle as well.'

'Ah.' Said Ethne.

'But worse than that, we've been asked to prepare for another house guest.' He paused before he could bring himself to say it. 'The Minister for Overseas Development.'

Even Lady Ethne's normally boundless optimism wilted.

***

The stream called The Run trickled, brightly, through a broken down corner of Jamestown, just beyond the Market Square. It had once been an open sewer bubbling and reeking under the ruined walls of what had served as the Sultan of Zanzibar's mansion during his exile. On the other side of the stream was island's long abandoned botanic garden, enclosing the rampant remains of a once great collection of plants of the sub tropical world. They pulsed with the humming of bees and other insects as they slowly strangled each other and made a bid for freedom over and through the crumbling walls.

No visitors normally came to the garden. Hadn't for fifty years since the last gardener had abandoned the unequal struggle with bloody minded nature. It was on a path to nowhere and one of the few quiet places in Jamestown. But that morning, just inside the archway that had once been the grand entrance and partially hidden by a tangle of bougainvillea two people were in heated conversation. The man, dressed in sharply pressed uniform, gesticulated, a piece of crumpled paper in his hand, and pointed back to the town. The woman, taller and wearing dark glasses and a tightly tied headsquare seemed to be trying to calm him down. After some minutes she took the paper and having read it, laid a hand on the man's arm and spoke to him slowly and deliberately. Without replying he turned away and headed back to Jamestown Square.

When Noriega had gone the woman walked a few feet further into the garden and lit a cigarette and leaned against a Eucalyptus tree, watching the sun piercing the canopy.

'Well he didn't seem very happy.' Florence Lacey had appeared from behind the wilderness of competing plants.

'Too used to shouting 'jump' and expecting people to go into orbit.' Dee Reeves carefully stubbed out her cigarette. 'But t'be fair to our little wind up generalissimo, Bloor's bein' a dick. Askin' for big bucks to tell us what he's got.'

'I thought you had enough dirt on him to scare him out of his grubby underpants.'

'So did I, but maybe he's de-cided he'll just stay here anyhow. Plenty of cheap booze and enough little Saint girls to massage his artistic temperament.'

Florence Lacey grimaced. 'And what has he given us for free?'

'Not much. Con-firmation of the harbour project, but we knew that anyhow. And a hint it's going to be used sooner rather than later.'

'Twenty Fifth. Three days.' Florence unfolded Hanrahan's note and handed it to Mrs. Reeves. 'Special cargo coming in on the Tinsley Challenger to coincide with Ship Day.'

'Mye,oh,mye.' Dee Reeves re-read the note. 'But still no names?'

'Well actually, yes. We have one. Came from some other

routine email traffic. It seems the British Embassy is getting ready for a Ministerial visit.' She paused for effect. 'John Prescott is coming in on the Challenger.'

'What the hell are they up to?' Said Dee Reeves, lighting another cigarette. 'Maybe Noriega was right. Maybe it's time we let him be a bit Panamanian with the good Mr. Bloor.'

***

'They used to call it the 'Lords' of the South Atlantic.' Lieutenant Shaffernacher was reading from a battered guide book to St Helena. He and Birtwistle were lounging in creaking rattan chairs on the verandah of the Francis Plain cricket pavilion; bamboo held together with sisal. 'It says that somewhere over there, just on the edge of the pitch, there's a deep gully with a waterfall. A fielder, trying to stop a six, went over backwards. Dead when he got to the bottom, but because there were only five overs to go they carried on with the game.'

'That's the spirit.' Said Birtwistle, looking out over the sports field that hung, shimmering between the mountains and the sea. He took another swig of water and returned the bottle to his pack. 'But we'd better push on if we're going to get somewhere near Kampala before stumps.'

They set off in the direction of the gully and started to clamber down to the lower ground. Near the top a heart shaped rock was split by the steam. As it fell it was caught by the wind off the Atlantic and turned into clouds of spray before reforming into a trail of water that plunged perhaps a hundred feet to the boulders below. By the time Birtwistle and the lieutenant were half way down they were soaked, but the water and the breeze were a merciful release from the stifling air of the plain.

Twenty minutes after they came out of the shadows of the cliff they were dry again and baking again. The climb out to what the map identified as Friar's Ridge was hampered by tall, thorny vegetation that dragged at their clothes and left scratches on their hands which began to itch. The lieutenant suggested what they really needed was a helicopter. That's what proper armies used. Birtwistle smiled and slashed at a particularly spiky bush and said that, in his experience, helicopters tended to be a bit on the noisy side for undercover operations. 'So will my screams be if I fall into another of these fucking clumps of God's razor wire.' Said the lieutenant with feeling.

By the time they arrived at the forest edge, at a point where they could see the ruin on the shoulder of Battery Hill that Birtwistle had identified as a possible place to hide away for the night, their decision to dispense with the much discussed, imaginary helicopter was fully vindicated. Someone had got to the old quarantine station before them. Where, once, sufferers from typhoid or TB had been brought to have a death with a view, fifty or sixty men sat about in the shade of the peeling walls. Birtwistle signed to the lieutenant to take cover and scanned the scene through his binoculars. Half the soldiers looked as if they'd been kitted out by an Oxfam shop; the other half by a fancy dress store. Perhaps ten of them were wearing what appeared to be blonde afro wigs. None of the uniforms matched. Five or six of them looked like Federation Peace Keepers' fatigues.

He recognised the jolly giant, Amin, immediately. He was standing legs planted apart and with his hands on his hips talking to a smaller man who, Birtwistle thought, looked a bit like Martin Luther King, but it could have been a trick of the low light. There was a third man, or at least the brigadier surmised it was a man, propped up on cushions in an ornate litter and being fussed round by an aged servant.

Amin clapped his hands and shouted an order and an NCO, who had a passing resemblance to the butler at the British Embassy, snapped to attention and started barking commands in costermonger cockney. Odder and odder. Birtwistle wondered if maybe he'd had too much sun.

The rabble of soldiers slowly got to their feet and sullenly shuffled in the dust. Birtwistle and the lieutenant worked their way closer to the buildings through a narrow belt of overgrown pine wood while the NCO valiantly attempted to make the soldiers look more like a platoon and less like the morning after a bad night in the shebeen.

'Restsured Imtinkin this am starting great campaign show Imperialis boss fellas biiig sprise..'

'If you go down to the woods today..' Birtwistle hummed under his breath as he watched Amin address his troops.

'Presdent Taylor am Emprer Bokassa been doin sensble ting Imtinkin make big dada commanderanchief. So.... I dress you today...'

'Not quite got the Montgomery touch.' Birtwistle whispered to the Lieutenant. 'But he's probably an altogether nicer person.'

'...Ashoo spreme commander. You do wat Imtinkin an I make you heroes o Africa. Heroes great black struggle gains powers ob whiteness you listnin.'

The soldiers looked as if they were listening but not receiving.

'We bin train fo dis momen Imtinkin so power Allah...'

There was a sharp tapping noise from the litter where Bokassa was rattling his cane on the gilded woodwork. What looked like a battery operated crucifix, faintly flashing neon red and with a hint of Parkinson's disease, appeared from under the heap of clothes.

'Power Allah wit forces Jees Chris on de lef flank bring fire from de sky on headswa enemies...'

'Hallelujah.' Taylor shouted, startling several of the gawping soldiers.

'Shaffernacher isn't by any chance a Jewish name?' Birtwistle asked the Lieutenant quietly, 'because if it was, we could have the full set.'

The lieutenant continued to stare open mouthed at the waving crucifix and shook his head.

'Pity.' Said Birtwistle.

'So what do we do now?'

'Well...' In the distance, Amin's oratorical pidgin took flight again. '...I think you'd better head back to town. British Embassy though. No point trying to talk to Reeves. He probably thinks he's

145

Luke Skywalker by now. Tell Jardine that everything's under control.'

Things didn't appear to be under control to Shaffernacher but he knew from experience that brigadiers moved in mysterious ways.

Birtwistle dusted off his uniform and straightened his beret. 'I think what President Amin needs more that anything else, except perhaps psychiatry, counselling and a speech therapist, is a professional second in command.' The brigadier stood up and strolled out of the wood. The lieutenant started to say something but then thought better of it and keeping his head down, set off in the direction of Jamestown.

CHAPTER THIRTEEN

'And Grace will be secretary.' Mugabe said with a flourish. The rest of the assembled company nodded agreement. The humble role of minute taker was the first thing they'd agreed about in three hours.

The main problem had been the voting system which had been a mystery to most of the participants. For half an hour, first one then another proclaimed their appointment to positions on the committee, only to be shouted down by everybody else. Eventually Gaddafi, who'd ruled himself out because he hoped not to be around for the committee's second meeting, suggested that elections were probably the answer. He filled the uncomfortable silence by saying that a tiny dose of democracy couldn't possibly do any harm so long as it was kept firmly in the hands of those present and not allowed to escape into the street.

The debate about who would be chairman had been particularly quarrelsome. It was only after six inconclusive shows of hands that Duvalier's attention disorder kicked in. He forgot to vote and Mugabe was elected by the narrowest of majorities.

Treasurer had also been a problem for obvious reasons. Stroessner, Mengistu and Aristide all made their pitch but it was Pinochet who eventually carried the day on the strength of a Swiss bank account chock full of gold bars. Mugabe would of course have been the natural choice had he not already been declared chairman.

Grace crossed her legs into secretary mode and sat poised with sharpened pencil to minute the inaugural meeting of the Presidential Action Committee.

The idea for the committee had sprung from Aristide and Duvalier's acrimonious meeting the previous day. Having started as a private Haitian grudge match, the exchanges had gradually drawn in shouted contributions from all and sundry. Within ten minutes the foyer of the Consulate Hotel had become the Jerry Springer Show. Stroessner was on his feet waving a podgy fist and protesting about some slight he'd once had to endure at a meeting with Pinochet in Chile. Noriega, red in the pineapple, was shouting at Stroessner about his habit of harbouring CIA troublemakers. Mengistu loudly (but slowly) berated Gadaffi about the lack of North African socialist solidarity and Duvalier and Aristide shouted and jabbed fingers and looked like dancing puppets. But when the Mugabe children joined in and started to throw angel cakes and macaroons around the room, Grace realised things had gone too far.

Her nails on a blackboard voice had cut through the clamour.

'Eeeenough. What sort of example is this for the children?'

The dictators subsided into silence.

'Where has gone the dignity of office? Where the vision of service to our people?'

They looked shiftily, one to another.

'Where has gone our sense of mission?'

The Jerry Springer show had begun to turn into an evangelical rally.

'The enemies are at the gate – not in this room.'

And then they saw each other in all their glory and they knew at that moment that they must unite for a greater good. Survival. Self interest. The golden dawn when the doors of a Presidential palace would swing wide to welcome them home. And then what fun they would have.

Robert Mugabe tapped a pencil against his glass and brought the meeting to order.

'Apologies?'

'I don't think so.' Said Grace.

***

It had been a jolly dinner. John Prescott had kept the company entertained with tales of his time as a waiter on the North Sea ferries.

'Aye, grand, sociable ships. With a bar.' Raising an eyebrow in Harry Tinsley's direction. 'Come on Harry. Wine's flowing like glue.' Harry Tinsley poured him another half glass. 'Dunt taste much better neither. aftertastes of barbed wire and 'orses 'ooves.'

'Aye, well mebbe you should have a word with the Ministry of Defeatism 'cos it's their stuff you're drinking. Sent down special when they heard we had a big knob on board.'

'Harriet, send them a snotty memo when we get back. Big knobs expect better. Anyoff, Harry are you sure you've got your bow doors shut? I'm sure I can feel a draught.'

'Don't have bow doors on proper ships. Just on the roll on, roll over jobs you used to like so much.'

'Nah, the only ones sailing the North Sea with their bow doors open were the lasses from Hull and Newcastle doing their fortnightly commute to the knockin' shops in Amsterdam.'

Inexplicably, Harriet excused herself and said she would go and compose the memo about the wine straight away.

'Aye, mebbe I'll have an early night, too, Harry.'

Tinsley watched the slim, retreating figure of the Minister's minder. 'You're not?'

'Course not. Every ejacumelation would be back with Campbell before you could say London Rubber Company.'

'Even I find that thought 'orrible.'

They walked together up to deck six and Prescott blew a kiss in the direction of Harriet's cabin before turning into his own.

Three hours later the ship was silent apart from the distant hum of electrical generation. Prescott looked out of the cabin porthole and saw they were sailing a flat and moonlit sea. He let himself out of the cabin and padded, barefoot along the corridor to the companionway. On deck five the wardroom was deserted and he stood for a few minutes listening at the top of the flight that led down to deck four. The hum was louder now but everything else was quiet. He went down slowly, stopping after each tread and approached the watertight door that cut off deck four from the rest of the ship. The metal handle moved easily and he gently pulled the heavy door open a couple of inches and looked inside. Two soldiers, wearing the insignia of the SAS, sat by a door half way along the brightly lit corridor. Both were asleep, their guns across their knees. For a minute, he wondered if he could get to the door without waking them but thought they'd more than likely be able to hear his heart pounding. Where he was standing it was drowning out the hum of the generator. He'd started to push the door closed when he heard another sound. Someone in the room was talking. The voice rose and fell. A chant, a moan? It tailed away but when the voice started again, low and menacing this time, there were odd words he could just make out – revenge, database, budget, evil and clearest of all, Bush and Blair spoken as a deep, drawn out threat. One of the soldiers stirred. Prescott silently closed the door and tiptoed back to his cabin. Once inside, he stood, breathing heavily, with his back to the door and carefully thought through what he'd seen and heard. And having thought it through, he thought - what the fuck does that all mean?

***

When Birtwistle had stepped out of the wood, only Charles Taylor had noticed at first. And all he could do was look, open mouthed, at Amin and tilt his head a couple of times in the brigadier's direction. At first Amin thought his comrade from Liberia was having some sort of seizure and he stopped in mid ramble and looked him up and down.

'Mr. President. Commander in Chief.' Amin turned and saw Birtwistle strolling towards him. 'What a coincidence. I was thinking about you no more than an hour ago at the Federation cricket ground. Thinking we really must see you lead out the Ugandan national team. Thought we might organise a friendly with a Joint Staffs side.'

'You shouldna be this way wandrin Imtinkin Brigadier.'

Birtwistle could have sworn he caught the hint of a Scottish accent. 'Oh, just taking the air. At a loose end.' Then close to Amin he turned his back on Taylor and said confidentially 'By the way, the nurse lady. Had a word. Should be in Kampala next week.'

Amin beamed. 'Bouncy, bouncy.' He slapped Birtwistle on the back. 'Always Imtinkin can do business widda proppa British

150

offassers undastand big man's app-etite.'

And with luck feed him just enough to do what they want. That's the way it always used to work, thought Birtwistle.

'This my friend - biiig man.' Amin turned back to Taylor. 'Him get big daddy outa Merican jail.'

'Yes, the Americans can be a bit uncivil.' Said Birtwistle. 'Probably weren't a British colony for quite long enough to have their rough edges knocked off.'

Amin nodded thoughtful agreement and introduced Taylor who was still gawping and then the heap of rags in the litter. Bokassa couldn't put his head back far enough to get up past the brigadier's chest. A croak came from the crumple of blankets. 'Faites veaux jeaux, as we used say. Wha's your game, Mr. big man?' The voice in the laundry heap faded away.

Amin cut in, already relishing the thought of pneumatic nights. "Imtinking missa big brigdeer join us. I'm promised him feelmarshall. We sit down talk stratjy. Show Merica they verra little men what dey be.'

Oh, that'll be a challenge, thought Birtwistle. Thinking of something offensive to say about our dearest friends and constant allies? But he gave it his best shot.

Reeves had gone doolally. Rumsfeld, too. Then he let his imagination kick in. They planned to crush Uganda; invade Liberia. He stopped short of nuking the Central African Republic on the principle that even Amin might think that was over the top. But by the time Birtwistle had finished inventing the gory details of the Reeves and Rumsfeld battle plan, he had them eating out of his hand. Only the butler from the British Embassy, now incongruously kitted out as garrison sergeant major in the Ugandan Special Forces, was looking at him rather strangely.

The sun settled orange on the far horizon. 'Think the men should turn in for the night, Sarnt Major. Long march tomorrow.'

Momo saluted and marched them to the roofless isolation ward that would be their billet. When they'd gone Birtwistle outlined his plans.

151

Later, the light of the campfire flickered on the faces of three Heads of State being served supper by the shuffling Chef de Cabinet of an African Emperor. Never Never Land, Birtwistle thought, as he excused himself to check the sentries. Predictably they were asleep and he left them that way. But he found Momo awake, standing in the moonlight shadow of one of the old buildings. Birtwistle beckoned him to follow and they skirted the camp in a wide circle until they were in the shelter of the strip of pinewood. They stood in silence for a few minutes watching the fire lit tableau a couple of hundred yards away.

'So what are you doing here?' Birtwistle asked.

Momo explained how he'd been sent by Lady Jardine to find out what he could but that, by accident, he'd got a bit closer to the action than he'd planned.

'Yes, me too it seems. And we seem to have a bit of a challenge on our hands.'

'Not half,' said Momo. 'Amin's planning to take the mail ship and storm the Embassies. He wants the Embassy staff to carry him on their shoulders through the streets. That'll keep the hernia wards busy for a bit. He's off his fucking trolley. Begging your pardon, sir.'

'No problem. Couldn't have put it better myself, sarnt major.'

Birtwistle thought for a moment and then ran through his alternative plan and, when he'd finished, told Momo to scarper back to the butler's pantry. 'And make sure Sir Henry does it exactly by the book or I could end up looking really rather silly.'

When Momo had gone Birtwistle retraced his steps and emerged out of the darkness into the circle of light around the fire. 'Everything seems peaceful.'

'Then we play dis game special ting.' Said Amin, opening up a board and laying it on the camp table.

Now this really is going to be a real challenge, thought Birtwistle as, out of a linen bag, fell a clatter of Scrabble tiles.

***

'I'm not sure which one's more crazy, the one who's shouting his head off or the one sitting in the corner writing poetry.' Second Officer Willis was leaning over the chart table on the bridge of HMS Bellerophon.

'Have you read any of his poetry?' asked Captain Pertwee, smoothing a bit of paper covered in pencil scrawl on the table. 'Listen to this. He insisted on writing one for me so I could zee de light.'

He launched into it.
Measure your steps, your hand's twists
That spear you throw is mad
The landscapes awaiting it are full of no names and no reason.
Something like a chill is nesting within you
That spear, that stretched arm, glows in your head

'He gets my vote,' said Pertwee. 'And he's a psychiatrist by profession. And you know the definition of a psychiatrist –a doctor who's gone mad.'

'Still, I was amazed how good his English is.'

'I know the English think all the bad guys are Johnnie Foreigner but I think you'll find English speakers sometimes go crackers, too. This one learned his doing medical training in the States. Where he learned genocide and mass murder is anybody's guess. Sarajevo finishing school. Srebrenica academy of the arts."

'He was bloody good at playing hide and seek, though. What was it – twelve years on the run?'

'If he was on the run. Five million reward and nobody turns him in. Not one greedy Serbian who'd take the money. Doesn't make sense. I reckon we've had him banged up all along.'

'So why didn't we just hand him over to the court in the Hague?'

'Maybe he knows where the bodies are buried?'

'Likely,' said Willis. 'There were plenty of them. They'd be hard to miss.'

'I mean some of the mistakes we maybe made that would be a bit embarrassing if they came out in open court. I don't know. Maybe the government in Montenegro was getting twitchy. Maybe rumours were getting about. Maybe some of his sidekicks were planning to spring him. So we collect him from a bunch of shady characters – spooks, CIA, MI6, who knows – pick him up off the Montenegran coast and whisk him away to an island in the sun.'

'Lot of maybe's,' said Willis. 'Why didn't we just knock him off? No shortage of mass graves to pop him into.'

'Because we're not Johnnie Foreigner, of course. And talking of courses, Mr. Willis, I think it's time we went easy on the international jiggery pokery and got back to our day jobs. We have a landfall which needs to be timed to perfection.'

Three decks below, Radovan Karadzic, tall, handsome and with the trademark shock of casually pushed back hair that had graced thousands of newspaper photographs and wanted posters in the past twelve years, picked up his pencil and created another dreadful poem.

As he finished, the commotion started again in the next cabin. The shouts and the banging on the door. The man making the noise was flushed, the red of his neck contrasting sharply with the white roll neck jumper. His hair and beard were flecked with grey but he still looked younger than his alter ego, appearing twice daily in a courtroom in Baghdad. After twenty minutes of the din echoing through the metal corridors of the ship, two guards and two medical orderlies unlocked the door and barged into the cabin. The man continued to shout and struggle as he was restrained against the wall and given an injection in his arm.

Within five minutes Saddam 'the crusher' Hussein was dreaming of walking in the gardens of his palace on the banks of the Tigris, a latter day Nebuchadnezzar, a virgin on each arm and oil pouring from the marble fountains.

He thanked the guards, shook hands with the medical orderlies and asked if they'd be so kind as to send in a packet of Doritos, a bowl of Raisin Bran and Tariq Aziz to see him. When he had the cabin to himself again he motioned to his Deputy Prime Minister to take a seat across the table and for an hour dealt with a busy agenda of international affairs. American sanctions, chemical weapon manufacture, relations with Iran, reprisals in the lands of the Kurds. Then, sighing, he closed the imagined folder on the desk and said he had a chapter of his new romantic novel to write and that, later, he'd be grateful if Tariq Aziz would join him for a viewing of the film The Old Man and the Sea, Ernest Hemingway being the only writer who could compete with his own, considerable talents.

When Aziz had gone Saddam slept and didn't notice the return of the orderlies who bustled round him. A side effect of the tranquilliser was that Saddam Hussein al-Majd al-Tikriti had peed his pants.

***

So, too, had Theo Bloor but it was fear rather than chemical tranquillity that had caused it.

Noriega had found him at his usual table in the White Horse and said they should go somewhere quieter where they could deal with the matter of payment away from prying eyes. The general set off into the maze of dark alleyways behind Main Street and Bloor followed unsteadily, occasionally bouncing off the walls. He didn't notice the two men who were following him at a distance. Noriega stopped at the door of what appeared to be some sort of warehouse close to the harbour. It was in complete darkness and a neuron of common sense fired through Bloor's alcoholic haze. He turned away, but as he stumbled the two men caught him by both arms and dragged him inside.

'So, I understand from Ahna you wish to do a deal. She mentioned a verra large sum 'o money.'

Bloor had been dumped on a chair in the middle of the dusty room and Noriega was shining a torch in his face. Theo looked nervously around trying to see where the other two men were standing.

'Yes, I do have shome information.'

'And we already have a deal, Mr Bloo-er. A deal with no mention of money.'

"I've already given the infomashun to fulfil that deal. This is different.'

Noriega cracked him on the side of the head with the heavy torch and one of the other men came up behind him and put an arm tight round his throat. That was when Bloor wet himself. The beam of the torch moved down to illuminate the spreading patch of damp.

'I don think you're cut out for these kind 'o works missa Blooer.' Noriega chuckled as Bloor's head fell forwards and he said 'Oright'.

It was done and dusted in a couple of minutes. Bloor gave Noriega the name. With no further quibble he told him how he came to hear it – a drunken conversation in the Standard with a Saint who happened to be related to someone who knew a crewman on one of the Tinsley ships. And then the fat man was dumped in the alleyway. When Noriega and his men had gone Bloor was sick down his waistcoat and the smells of vomit and whisky and urine mingled as Bloor struggled to his feet and staggered away in the direction of the Embassy. That night the industrial strength air freshener in his bedroom fought a losing battle.

CHAPTER FOURTEEN

The Foreign Secretary lay back in a deck chair with his eyes closed and listened to the clack of mallet on ball. The Prime Minister was about to notch up his second spectacular croquet defeat of the afternoon – this time at the hands of Alistair Campbell.

'You really ought to take up politics instead.' Said the scourge of the NUJ as he tapped a ball, arrow straight, to the peg. 'Not as competitive a game.'

'At least in politics you meet a nicer class of scoundrel.' Said Blair huffily, handing over a ten pound note as they walked back across the lawn.

'Awfully bad luck.' The Foreign Secretary was holding his winnings up to the light as if to check the note wasn't counterfeit. 'Think I'll run this one past the Treasury. But look on the bright side, Prime Minister. In twenty four hours you're going to be the darling of the democratic world.'

'Or on Rumsfeld's hit list.' Campbell grinned as he poured himself a glass of lemonade.

'That's a remark in singularly bad taste, Alistair. Especially as we all know there are more out of control crazies in the CIA than in your average hospital for the criminally insane.'

The autumn sun reflected from the windows of the great house, yellow to gold. The Prime Minister normally looked forward to the time he spent at his country retreat, away from the bear pit of Whitehall, but that weekend, even at Chequers, he felt uneasy about the political storm that was brewing.

He turned back from watching the sunlight dancing in the mullioned windows. 'We've really got to get our story straight. It's all very well us making the grand announcement but what do we say when America stops spluttering and starts briefing every journalist on the planet about Mugabe and Amin?'

'Easy.' Campbell leaned back in his deck chair with his hands behind his head. 'We just tell the truth.'

'Well, isn't that's an interesting departure.' Said the Foreign Secretary with a hint of sulphuric in his voice.

Campbell raised one eyebrow in his direction. 'We simply say we could no longer stand by while an ailing Mr. Mugabe destroyed Zimbabwe's economy, trampled on the democratic process, encouraged the murder of white farmers and terrorised his starving people. We've merely taken him into protective custody. How could any sane person disagree?'

'If you look very closely there's a very big and very dangerous assumption three words from the end of that remark,' said the Foreign Secretary. 'And of course no-one will notice that the chap we've backed as Mugabe's replacement – the one black man in Africa who doesn't think we're white colonial oppressors - has offered us huge compensation for previous nationalisations and extensive trade guarantees?'

'Not straight away they won't. And by the time they do, news about Mugabe will be appearing twice daily at your local fish and chip shop.'

'And how do we explain Amin?' Blair sounded weary.

'Caught him hatching a plot to stage a coup he hoped would return him to power in Uganda. Very convenient for us; very embarrassing for his Saudi hosts. Last thing they wanted was a mad, murdering muslim on the loose. (Ah, those were the days). Could give Islam a bad name, old boy. So we get a thumbs up and free oil vouchers from the Saudi Royal Family and grudging thanks from all the other countries that are crapping themselves about the spread of Islamic fundamentalism.'

'And not a mention of us, rather than the Chinese, getting our stickies on Uganda's copper and cobalt reserves.'

'Never knew they had any, Prime Minister,' said Campbell. 'Honest.'

'Please don't go over the top, Alistair.'

158

'There's the little matter of Radovan Karadzic.' The Foreign Secretary loved saying Radovan Karadzic, forming the words as if he was describing a particularly rich winter pudding.

'Another win, win. We were clever enough to catch him. Nobody will ever know precisely when and we're just hanging onto him somewhere safe and well away from his rabid Serbian supporters until the court in The Hague has had time to go through the three lorry loads of documents about his war crimes we've managed to assemble and are just about to deliver. With luck Karadzic will be about 103 by the time they've sorted out the legal arguments.'

Blair wasn't quite sure whether to nod or shake his head. 'And what do we say about Bokassa if anybody should happen to mention him?'

'If anybody should happen to remember him, even. No, he's a bit tricky, like Duvalier. As you know...' Campbell checked for signs of recognition but none surfaced. '...we're holding them as a favour to the French because they'd rather nobody heard about the foreign armaments backhanders and sweeteners a certain President of France used to fund his political campaigns. Trade off, after a decent interval they give way a bit on reform of the Common Agricultural Policy. I always said at the time it was a naff deal. You should never mix agriculture and real life. But we're stuck with it and because the Americans hate the fucking French they might be tempted to lob the odd rock into the lakes at Versailles to see where the ripples go.'

'Hate is such a …. dysfunctional word, Alistair.' The Foreign Secretary intervened like a footnote. 'Mistrust has so many more diplomatic nuances.'

Campbell, like most readers of works of popular history, skipped the footnote.

'But I'm not too worried because, bottom line, the Americans have more to lose than anybody else. If they brief against us, just imagine what tasty little morsels *we* can throw to the vultures. They've got at least four of their favourite neighbourhood psychos banged up in the same place – Noriega, Stroessner, Pinochet and

Taylor. By my reckoning...' he feigned counting on his fingers '...responsible for about three or four million dead between them – rough and dirty figures – and that was when the good ol' bible belt US of A was backing them to the bloody hilt. And I choose my words advisedly. No wonder they're trying to make them disappear. If any one of them started running off at the mouth it would take a bit of the greasy polish off the Republicans' campaign before the mid term elections. Fuck them, actually. Nothing the Democrats like better than a good dictator to be able to wave under the noses of a gullible electorate on the principle that a whiff of dictator, like a whiff of smelling salts soon brings people to their senses.'

The Foreign Secretary looked as if he was about to introduce a Foreign Office semantic quibble but was mown down as Campbell motored on.

'And they've got Aristide. Why is anybody's guess. I reckon they were planning to arrest the Mayor of Honolulu for gross indecency with a grass skirt and the CIA got the wrong island. And to top it all off they're playing now you see him, now you don't with Saddam Hussein. What's that all about?'

'Well it would be jolly embarrassing if the Mad Mahdi and his men walked into the court in Baghdad and liberated him,' said Blair. 'And on the Americans' present track record Muffin the Mule could probably manage that.'

'O.K., so they want to keep Saddo tucked up safe, I can see that. And so they just take over the system that's already worked hunky dory for ten years. American Equity signs up Saddam's national theatre company of look-alikes. Sixty nine of them I think there were at the last count.'

"Sensible, I'd have thought Alistair. If the system's working why bother to fix it,' said the Foreign Secretary, determined to re-take a little bit of Foreign Office ground.

'Except for one thing.'

The Foreign Secretary's position was overrun again.

'Even under Iraqi law you can't try an actor who's playing the part of a mass murderer for the crimes a real mass murderer who just happens to look like him carried out. Well I don't think you can.'

'So why *have* the American's done it?' The Foreign Secretary sounded genuinely interested.

'Didn't think it through. Probably came out of one of Dubyah's brainstorming sessions. And there's a fearsome thought. Probably the same one that screwed Kyoto, appointed Dick Cheney Presidential small arms advisor and threatened to nuke Iran, like as not.'

'So let me get this right.' said Blair, the thought coalescing as he spoke it. 'The Americans *want* the world to know that Saddam's been smuggled out of the country because then the insurgents won't bother to free the one in Baghdad?'

'No, Tony.' Advisor become carer. 'I'm assuming the real one is on the Bellerophon as we speak. And the last thing the Americans want is for anybody to know that.'

'But. Sorry if I'm being a bit dim here, but what happens if al Sadder and Sadder or whatever he's called blows away the one in Baghdad?'

'They've still got 68 left. Saddam seriously injured in attack. American medical expertise brought him round. Expected to make full recovery. Six months later a pale and drawn Saddam is back in court.'

'And the one getting a tan on St. Helena?'

'I'd imagine that when the Branagh of Baghdad has been tried and sentenced, they'll take the real one back for the final curtain call. String him up. One way ticket to virgin land. Or whatever Iraq's caring, sharing, politically impartial legal system eventually decides. And they've still got enough spare Saddam's to be able to do the appeals process, which of course will also decide he should be strung up.'

Blair looked at Campbell with some something approaching horror. 'But surely we'd have to oppose the death penalty. We couldn't just send him back to be executed. That's barbaric. And worse than that it would cause a most awful flurry with the Fabians.'

'Tony, if we do the job right the bloody Fabians won't even know we've got him. And what they don't know won't hurt them.'

And then as an afterthought. 'And anyhow, don't forget it would be Gordon having his ankles savaged by then.'

Blair looked mollified and he and the Foreign Secretary sat in silence for a bit, seemingly enjoying the autumn afternoon.

Campbell eventually broke the silence.

'And how about this to cheer you up. When it's all done and dusted, what do you think the Iraqis will do with 68 Saddam lookalikes, or however many have survived the hit squads?' He cocked is head on one side. 'Another shipload for the Bellerophon, I reckon.' He sat back and let his imagination take him to the dusty streets of Jamestown – whatever they looked like – and everywhere there were little groups of Saddam Hussein's chatting together about their greatest performances and comparing their best reviews.

***

By the time Momo got back to Jamestown he realised why he'd given up soldiery and taken to butlering instead. The journey by night across the hills had been almost as strenuous as English lessons. His Ugandan uniform was ripped down one sleeve. The sole was loose on one of his boots. Samples of the various vegetations he'd encountered along the way had attached themselves to buckles and buttons. And he was limping badly, having fallen thirty feet into one of the overgrown gullies that had appeared in his path. Or, to be more precise, hadn't appeared in his path. Fortunately, when he disappeared into one of them and hit the bottom it was covered with a dense carpet of low bushes which broke his fall rather than his neck. But he most certainly didn't look a pretty sight as he limped into Sir Henry Jardine's study.

'Think perhaps I'll leave comments about dress code to another occasion,' was the Ambassador's jolly greeting as he pulled out a chair and suggested Momo took the weight off his feet before he fell over. 'Look almost as bad as that awful man Bloor but he had less bloody excuse. He got in a mess just walking back from the pub.'

Momo glanced in Lady Ethne's direction and she beamed sympathetically. 'At least Momo appears drier and smells rather better for which much thanks.'

The butler back from manoeuvres wondered what the hell they were talking about but the wondering soon faded in the after effects of the first mouthful of scotch from the half pint glass Sir Henry had thrust into his hand.

'We've already had a message from Birtwistle that everything's under control – whatever that means. American Lieutenant called Shaffernutter…'

'Knacker, dear. Shaffer-knacker.'

'Well whatever he was called he got back looking a bit like you. Except, of course, he was white and the dirt showed rather more.' Sir Henry chuckled at his little joke and proposed a toast to political incorrectness. Momo grimaced and pretended it was a twinge from his sprained ankle. He told them what he'd discovered and outlined Birtwistle's plan. When he'd finished Sir Henry picked up the telephone and called Major Harding. 'Better pop over, Major and as Ambassador Reeves is still fighting Custer's last stand in his broom cupboard, you'd better bring Schweppes…'

'Schwarz, dear.'

'You'd better bring Shwarts with you as well.'

When he came off the telephone he muttered 'Can't for the life of me understand why these Americans have to give themselves such bloody silly names.' And Lady Ethne said, 'In the meantime, Momo, I think I'd better take a peek at that ankle.' And Momo quickly downed the rest of the whisky.

***

While the Indians rode, whooping in circles, round the Little Bighorn three floors below, Dee Reeves was quietly letting Florence Lacey and General Noriega into her room from the Embassy's back stairs.

'Well, aint things starting to pop.' Said Mrs Reeves after she'd poured them all a glass of wine. 'Californian I'm afraid. Some Embassy entertaining rules you just aint allowed to bend.'

'Unlike having spies in your drawing room.' Florence Lacey

chuckled.

'Let's just leave the spying to that nice Mr. Bond, Florence. Just as long as the world keeps thinking you need a big dick and a chevvy with rockets up its fanny to do the job, it makes life soh much easier for the rest of us.' Mrs. Reeves looked over her spectacles at the General.

Noriega raised his glass. 'And as we know, ladies, one man's spy is another's martyr of the revolution.'

'Oh, I do hope not.' The keeper of the regalia gave a pouting grimace. 'That sounds very messy.'

'Yes, let's go easy on the revolutionary stuff, Manuel,' Dee Reeves said, matter of fact. 'I know old habits die hard but, as I keep telling you, we're doing nothin' so exciting. A little low key exercise in international administration and public relations. That's all.'

Noriega proposed a toast to 'Information and the embarrassment it can cause' and they settled down to business.

Dee Reeves ran through the schedule. 'Latest news about Bellerophon?'

'Last heard of, running on time.' Said Florence.

'So, off Jamestown eleven o'clock local. And we won't have heard about Challenger.'

'Nothing. Radio silence. But we've just got to assume it's still working to the same ETA at Turk's Cap.'

'Bit of luck you doing Ship Day. Couldn't have planned for that if we'd tried.'

'Except I've just *nothing* to wear, my dear.' Florence looked down. 'Don't think I'd fit into Sir Henry's outfit, somehow. An aged dressmaker far end of Main Street is running up a frock coat and silly plumed hat as we speak.'

'And won't you just look the Broadway star.'

'Just hope I get off Broadway in one piece. Not sure if you can get Kevlar underwear at the Jamestown haberdashery.'

Noriega nodded, appreciatively. He'd always been partial to women in uniform although he couldn't immediately remember having had one who was wearing a silly plumed hat and Kevlar knickers at the time.

By the time he'd managed to drag himself away from conquests past and back to the meeting, Dee Reeves was outlining the diversionary plans for Jamestown which would keep the security forces busy for the vital hour after HMS Bellerophon's passengers had disembarked. 'Seventy five men which should be enough to make a bit of a bang. Amin thinks it's going to be 'de twilight dis imperial stuff himtinkin'. By the time we've got what we want and slipped back into our day jobs and he's left taking the rap, him better be 'tinkin' again.'

Noriega gave a reedy chuckle.

'And in the meantime Sir Henry has been given just enough clues to make sure he takes it seriously.' said Florence. 'The pressure in his alcohol system is probably rising already.'

'So what about Turk's Cap?' Dee Reeves turned her scarlet lipped smile on Noriega.

'Myzelf and three men. No problem. In. Out. An' then how you say – wag it all about.'

'Waggle it round the whole wide world, General. But remember you aint gonna have a lot of time. I'm guessing the announcement from London will be at noon, just in time for the lunchtime bulletins and more important, the American breakfast shows. You've got to be finished before that.'

'One half hour. Thaz all we need. And we've ready laid our own little diversione. We gonna have fireworks.' He raised his glass again. 'Like fourth of July.'

***

There was no sparkle in Birtwistle's rag tag army. It was advancing with defeat in every step. Having mislaid its Sergeant Major it had reverted to sullen shuffling. When Momo's disappearance had been discovered that morning Amin had gone into near earth orbit. Armed with a machete he went storming about the camp, searching the buildings and beheading patches of scrub. Several soldiers, squatting to relieve themselves in the bushes, had the closest of close shaves.

'He Bagandabastard.' Swish. Another thorn bush met its maker. 'Knew it all long Baganda fella traitor.' Swoosh. A clump of flax exploded. 'Bagandaman no bag and a no balls big fella catchim.' Slash.

Of course, those'll be the Brixton Baganda's, Birtwistle thought. He was sitting with his feet up by the remains of the fire as Amin, self appointed Prince of the Kakwa, re-fought Uganda's tribal wars.

On the other side of the fire Charles Taylor was raging, too, but in a more measured, Old Testament, fire and brimstone sort of way, calling down everyone from Abraham to Zachariah on Momo's head. 'And may the pawa, the pawa of the Holy Spirit seeeel his miserable mouth.'

'No problem there, Mr President,' Birtwistle had said while giving his own mouth a brief respite from its attempts to make an impression on the charred but tough goat meat that was the only breakfast on offer. 'Knows nothing. Probably just homesick.'

'He knows where we are.' Spoken like the voice of God in an amateur mystery play or any production featuring Brian Blessed.

'Ah, but we're not going to be here for long and he doesn't know where we're going and he doesn't know what we're going to be doing when we get there.' He made another failed attempt at the goat before throwing it into the fire. 'And anyway I'm sure The Almighty will, as ever, be on the side of the righteous.'

'Allelujah.' And then as a practical afterthought. 'Meantime I'll be praying to the Saints, our helpmates in times of trouble, that our AWOL Sergeant Major gets real sick not just home sick.'

'Maybe tomorrow you could try the same thing with the cook.' But Taylor didn't hear him. He was already communing with the Saints.

Birtwistle thought that of all his new-found associates he much preferred Bokassa. At least he just dribbled.

After about twenty minutes Amin's notoriously short memory had kicked in. Momo was all but forgotten, the cook was slapped about a bit for not knowing how to cook goat and Amin peed on the camp fire. 'Kakwa tradition stop ebil spirits follow him trail'. By ten o'clock Birtwistle got the show on the road.

Except, of course there was nothing you could describe as a road anywhere in the vicinity and the men strung out behind him certainly bore no resemblance whatsoever to the Greatest Show on Earth. But he still found himself humming the stirring tunes he remembered from boyhood trips to the circus. Ringmaster Birtwistle with his troupe of clowns.

Roll of drums. 'Hand now. Fifty feet above your very 'eads the three Hamin's will attempt a feat never seen befowah…Passin' from trapeze to trapeze while hall the time jugglin' with live 'and grenades. Hand for their finahale the hemperor Bokassa – who's a real hemperor from Hafrica by the way – will catch one of the haforementioned grenades in 'is teeth.'

Birtwistle smiled to himself and wondered if madness was catching. Maybe he'd picked up a dose of whatever it was had sent Amin off his trolley. But as that was, reportedly, syphilis he fervently hoped he was suffering from nothing more serious than lack of food, the side effects of inedible goat.

The old quarantine station on the shoulder of Isaac's hill wasn't more than five miles from Jamestown along the coast but Birtwistle had decided to take a more roundabout route. Even though the soldiers already looked as if they were ready for bed rather than battle he thought it no bad thing to tire them out a bit more. So he cut inland along Friar's Ridge heading for a hilly, wooded area marked on his map as Scotland. That should make Amin feel at home, he thought when he saw the name. And who knows, maybe this is the Scotland where Mary Queen of Scots really ended up rather than in bits in Westminster Abbey. And with the Colony's grip on reality being what it was, maybe she was still here, wandering about in her scarlet petticoats with her head under one arm and her Skye terrier under the other. And wouldn't that be a royal match made in heaven? Nippers with Amin's looks and Mary's temperament. Even more scary the other way round.

167

When Birtwistle looked back he saw the column had ground to a halt again, this time because Bokassa's litter was wedged in a narrow gully. Amin had his uses. When six straining soldiers failed to shift the Imperial blockage, one wrench from Big Daddy's hand got it moving. It also nearly tipped the bundle of Imperial rags into a culvert and ripped off a section of termite ridden Imperial gilding. But at least they were moving again and by now heading northwest over Red Hill. In the dense woodland beyond it Birtwistle at one point realised he'd taken them in a complete circle and that they were passing the distinctive ruins of a hut for the second time but nobody apart from him seemed to notice. Neither did anyone comment on the view that opened up through the trees over Donkey Plain where pride of place in this supposedly empty land was taken by the Jamestown municipal rubbish dump. It was the only advance the Brigadier had ever experienced that felt like a retreat.

By seven in the evening the soldiers were looking even more revolting than normal. There were mutinous mutterings back along the line and Amin was hard at work raising morale by threatening to personally 'bloway' the next man who complained. At eight, having successfully turned a five mile walk into a fifteen mile route march, Birtwistle brought them to the old quarry at the head of Breakneck Valley where he planned to camp for the night. It would be no more than a couple of hours from there to the helicopter landing pad on Ladder Hill where they had to be by mid morning.

The mood in the camp wasn't improved by Birtwistle banning camp fires in case the smoke could be seen from Jamestown and more important, in case the cook decided to fire harden another goat. But weariness soon settled the grumbling and before long the only sound in the darkness was the occasional rattling of Bokassa's pill bottles and Amin's surprisingly gentle snoring and Taylor keeping God up late again. Birtwistle sat back against the quarry face and watched the shooting stars and thought he hadn't had as a good a time since that pompous buffoon Trelawny had fallen off his horse during Trooping the Colour. Idi Amin, the Garrison Sergeant Major, marched out from the central arch of Horseguards followed by four

NCO's carrying a large black cooking pot. Amin apologised to Her Majesty, picked up Trelawny like a scraggy chicken and popped him in the pot which was already simmering.

'How you bin likin' him cooked missa Queen woman?'

'One prefers one's officers well done. And as you obviously have extensive experience of colonial matters, Mister Amin, tell one, who is that little man with the Queen of Tonga?'

And the command 'Eyes Right' rang out and number six guard, at that moment marching past the dais with bones in their noses and wearing loincloths and suspenders, shouted with one voice

'LUNCH'.

But that may have been a dream.

***

John Prescott woke with a start and for a moment couldn't work out where he was in the half light. But then the banging on the cabin door started again and he focused on the porthole circle gleaming dimly through the thin curtain. He was lying on the bed fully dressed, if his eye lashing outfit could be so described.

'Hang about.'

He swung his legs onto the floor and rubbed his eyes. It had been a long and liquid lunch to ease the boredom of the long hours at sea, during which he and Harry Tinsley had set the world and Hull to rights.

'That's some fist you've got there, lassie,' he said sleepily to Harriet who bustled in and laid her papers on the cabin table. 'Pity your poor boyfriend if ever you caught him fragrantly delicto. And, anyoff it's a poor do if the Deputy Prime Minister can't have a kip of an afternoon. Bed's not as comfy as the front bench but at least in here it's not like sleeping in a bloody zoo.'

'Sorry to disturb you, but I did leave you for a couple of hours before dragging you back to work.'

'Like I said, hang about till I get a drop of re-hydration.' He

169

threw back several glasses of water. 'I'm sure that wine's made in a chemical plant in Runcorn. Probably use it for taking rust off battleships. The stuff they put in bottles is when they've made it too strong. Eats through the hulls.'

'It's going to be a bit busy in the morning so I just thought we should run through the arrangements.' She pushed a sheet of paper in front of him as he sat down. 'We'll be disembarking our passenger at eleven and when the transfer ashore has been completed you have to contact Downing Street for instructions. The radio coms. Officer will be setting up a secure circuit via the Admiralty. The British Ambassador will be meeting us on the quay and when he's supervised the unloading of the secure cargo the plan is he'll drive us across to Jamestown. Should take a couple of hours but we've had a message from London that there could be a spot of bother there – all under control apparently but it might still delay us. That could mean we'll have to postpone one of our meetings until the following day...'

'Hang on again. Afore we start getting down to what frock I'm going to wear for the St. Helena W.I. reception, this here passenger, let's talk about him for a minute. For starters how come I can't meet him?'

'We don't know it is a 'him'. And it's not just you. Nobody's met the person except the two guards and they've been shut up in the same corridor since they came aboard.'

'Well I do know it's a *him* because I've heard *him*.' Prescott rocked back in his chair and put his hands behind his head.

'And how, exactly, did you do that, Minister.' Harriet suddenly more frosty.

'Oh, just natural curiosity let's call it. To get on in the Labour Party you've got to be good listening at doors. Only way to head off being shafted.'

'But Mr. Tinsley warned you about going to deck four.'

And how did she know that, thought Prescott? Maybe there were a few more doors he should be listening at. 'Harry's been

170

warning me about things for forty odd years – and I still haven't gone blind.'

'You really have to start taking advice more seriously, Minister. It's vitally important that things go smoothly tomorrow. I've been instructed by the Prime Minister personally that if Jolly John – his phrase of course, not mine – if Jolly John plays up or plays the fool I have the authority to have him…'

'What? Clapped in irons, keel hauled, made to walk the plank, thrown overboard? Very bloody democratic. Very New fucking Labour.'

'Restrained.'

'Nay, me and Mrs P have never been into that sort of kinky stuff. Messes up her hair. And I get a horrible allygemetic reaction to the handcuffs. But if that's what turns you on lass I've never been a man to turn down a challenge.'

'Just behave, Minister.' Harriet swept up her papers and headed for the door.

'Sorry I've been a bad lad.' Said Prescott, by now standing legs crossed and wringing his hands. 'Promise I'll be good till we get tomorrow out of the way.'

'Not before time. But just in case you're not, I'm sure Mr. Tinsley will have the odd cat o' nine tails in his punishment locker.'

'Ooh you are awful. But I like you.' Harriet raised her eyes and Prescott blew her a slobbery Dick Emery kiss as she disappeared into the corridor.

Much later, when Prescott padded in his stocking feet to the top of the companion way ladder to deck four and peeped over the rail he saw a crewman had been stationed outside the security door. But on his way back to his cabin, what he heard outside another door, this time on deck six, confirmed what he's suspected for some time - that Tony Blair was indeed a slice of boiled ham short of a funeral tea.

***

'No, Major Harding, we can not bring in reinforcements from either Ascension or Cape Town.' Sir Henry Jardine, diplomat, was about to explode.

'But, Sir Henry, we only have a security force of sixty men and you tell us you need ten of them for unspecified special duties. That leaves just..'

'Fifty. I may of course be wrong, Major, suffering as I do from the wholly inadequate education provided by Eton and Oxford, but humour me. Fifty is my best guess.'

'And the point I'm trying to make, Ambassador, is that I don't think that fifty men can guarantee the security of Jamestown on a Ship Day when we're faced with a rebel attack.'

'And what do you think, Mr Shwartz?' Sir Henry's patience twanged like an overstretched rubber band.

'Reckon the brigadier's plan seems to stack up. Bit risky splitting the fifty into two units but you can see where he's coming from. And we've got the tank.'

Sir Henry watched the rotations of Shwartz' mouth. He realised this was the first time anyone had ever dared chew gum in his office. Normally the Ambassador's response would have been withering, but this mouth was in active agreement so he let it be. 'Quite so, Mr Shwartz. Good to see the reputation of the American armed forces generated by such adventures as Vietnam and Iraq is, at least in part, ill founded.' That was as close to letting it be as he could manage. Shwartz briefly stopped chewing.

'Agreed, then.' Sir Henry closed the file on his desk. 'Mr Shwartz will take command of the high level unit and when you've stopped sulking, Major Harding, you'll be in charge of the Jamestown detachment. Both in position by 08.00 hours. My squad of ten with two landrovers to meet me here at six. Good afternoon gentlemen. And, Mr. Shwartz, I'd be eternally grateful if you could resist the temptation to leave your chewing gum on any part of the Embassy woodwork on the way out.' Shwartz' mouth fell open so far that it was the carpet rather than the woodwork that was immediately under threat.

Pike, on his way into the office, passed them at the door. 'Harding looks as if he's being sent to Dunkirk.'

'Bloody idiot. Often wonder who gets him dressed in the mornings. Still, beggars can't be choosers. If the powers that be have decided all we need here is a mentally retarded Major destined for promotion to his local labour exchange, who are we to argue?'

Pike unfolded the letter he was carrying. 'And just to put the icing on the afternoon's cake, Sir Henry, you'd better see this.' He passed it over and after a moment or two, the storm that had been threatening to break in the Ambassador's office for the past hour, at last arrived.

'Demands.'

'I read it more as 'requests', Ambassador.'

'Does the word 'demand' appear in this document, Mr. Pike, or does it not?'

'It does, but the overall tone is more conciliatory than that one word taken out of context would suggest…'

'The context, as you describe it, is that our distinguished, disreputable guests have decided to form an action committee. A *Presidential* action committee, no less, which is 'demanding' negotiating rights about everything from aid packages to overseas travel…'

'It's nothing we don't already pretend to do with them individually.'

'Don't interrupt, Mr. Pike.' Sir Henry left a pause into which to tempt Pike to jump. 'The difference here..' The paper in his hand became a white blur. '..is that they've settled their differences…'

'Oh that's very unlikely, Sir Henry, egomaniacs just don't mix….'

'Shut up, Pike.' Like a rumble of distant thunder. 'I suggest you keep your half digested psychological theories to spice up your pillow talk with Mrs. Reeves. Make a change from choosing bikinis together.' Snarled in a nah ne nah ne nah sort of way.

Pike blushed but bravely persevered. 'I was just trying to make the point, Sir Henry, that these are not clubbable people…'

'Well, don't.'

'Don't what, dear?' Lady Ethne breezed into the room and the barometer rose.

'The bloody lunatics are making a take over bid for the madhouse.' He waved the letter again and Ethne took it gently from his hand.

'Well hasn't Mr. Mugabe been a busy bully.' She smiled benignly. 'But credit where credit's due, Henry. No wonder he managed to hang onto power for so long if he can get this lot to agree to anything other than who should hold the keys to the Central Bank.'

'And to top it all they're demanding representation on the Joint Staffs. It's like having Hitler ex officio on Churchill's bloody war cabinet.'

'Of course that's out of the question. But in the meantime there's no harm sending Mr. Pike along to their next meeting to listen to their grievances, Henry. And won't that be a jolly afternoon for you, Richard?' She turned her benign smile on him but it didn't ease the horror of the thought. 'You can unveil some new Overseas Development Scheme that will reinvigorate their goat farming industries, or something equally distasteful, and of course all paid for through their favourite Swiss piggy bank. Sorry about the mish mash of animals, but I'm sure you get the idea, Richard.'

'I'd go easy on the piggy bank references with Gadaffi.' Said Henry. 'Don't think Muslims use them.' His storm was subsiding under Ethne's temperate meteorological influence and he headed for a drizzle of Talisker.

'No need to worry about Gaddafi, he's on the way out tomorrow on Bellerophon. That's what I popped in to tell you, dear. Message just in from London.'

Henry groaned. 'Not another. Thank God we're going to be up country. Jamestown pier's going to be like Euston bloody Station tomorrow. Flags going up and down faster that a hooers drawers, as my old theology teacher used to say.' Then to Pike in a tone of quite genuine sympathy. 'You and Florence are going to have your work cut out….'

Ethne coughed. 'But getting back to the silly Presidential

174

committee for just a moment. We also need to liberate a bit of information in the right quarters. Who's been getting what from whom. That sort of thing. And particularly how much more than the rest of them their respected chairman has been salting away. All *deliciously* untrue. But let's see how long the unity lasts.'

Sir Henry took his replenished glass to the window and looked down on Jamestown Main Square. It was emptying into a golden evening. On the pier, the statues on the two granite plinths were throwing long shadows, particularly the one brandishing a fist in the air. Ethne joined Henry at the window. 'Lovely, isn't it. But I think we should have an early night, dear. Busy day tomorrow.'

CHAPTER FIFTEEN

'It's going to be a bit basic this morning, to say the least.' Florence Lacey, in a frock coat which looked as if it had been made for somebody half as big again, was running through the final arrangements on the pier with Richard Pike. 'No Honour Guard, of course. They're playing at being proper soldiers instead. National anthems on tape.' Two large, grey speaker cones on stands pointed towards the quay. 'That will probably be a blessing. And Momo's been drafted in to help with crowd arrangements.' A workman was painting 'Bon Voyage, Mr. President' on the back of the 'Welcome Home Mr. President' banner.

'We really ought to install a bloody revolving door." Pike said in imitation of Sir Henry as he looked up at the statues on their granite plinths. The one of Saddam Hussein had seen better days. For one thing it was cut off below the knees and the once bulbous nose now had a flat end, acquired when it hit a Baghdad pavement, having been toppled by his adoring citizenry. The statue of Karadzic, as befitted a psychiatrist cum genocidal poet, was a modern work of unfathomable dreadfulness, all angles, cogs and rusty welding, that looked as if it had been created by Picasso's car mechanic.

'Are they going to be coming ashore individually or as a job lot?' Asked Pike, turning his head on one side to see if the statue made more sense from a different angle (it didn't) and as Florence fussed with her paperwork.

'Oh, no, one at a time. Standards, Mr. Pike, standards. We can't be letting ours slip just because they've mislaid theirs.' As she spoke, the prow of HMS Bellerophon eased into view round Munden's Point to the North West. 'That means we've got about twenty minutes. Let's just have a final canter through the protocols.'

'Before we do, I'd better let our local Rembrandt here know there's an 'e' in voyage.'

***

On cue, on the other side of the island, the Tinsley Challenger hove into view past Barn Point. The plumes on Sir Henry Jardine's hat were vibrating slightly as they registered the aftershocks of the Ambassador's bone shaking Land Rover ride to Turk's Cap.

'You have to concede it's impressive.' Said Lady Ethne looking out along the crisp, white concrete quay and then to the cliff face behind her into which had been driven a considerable tunnel, its entrance protected by tall, barred metal doors.

But Sir Henry wasn't in concessionary mood. 'Never enjoyed charades, even when the prize was strawberry ice cream from nanny Moffat and I certainly don't like them now when the reward is a crushed spine and bloody sunstroke courtesy of nanny Blair.' He reached for his hip flask and took a long swig of spinal embrocation and sun tan cream.

Five soldiers from the security detachment were deployed at the point where the unsurfaced road from the hill came out onto the quay. They were visibly wilting in the stifling heat. The other five, spaced along the quay itself to take the Challenger's mooring lines, at least had the benefit of an occasional and welcome touch of sea breeze.

All eyes were on the great wall of ship, topped with containers, which was turning in the bay to approach the harbour stern first. No-one noticed the four men keeping low among the rocks as they worked their way down from the ruined Dutch battery to take up positions near the edge of the cliff, overlooking the harbour sixty feet below them.

***

Against the odds, Birtwistle's stumbling rebel army had arrived with time to spare into the field of tall grass behind the helicopter pad. Perhaps they'd moved unusually fast because the grumbling soldiers had been told they could have breakfast when they got to Jamestown. 'Big Mac all him trimmings,' Amin had promised at the early morning muster, omitting to mention the fact that the nearest fast food outlet, unless you particularly fancied tucking into a raw yam, was some twelve hundred miles away. Bokassa, as befits an Emperor of Africa, had been kitted out with his bib and was being spoon fed gruel and brightly coloured pills by his ever present Chef de Cabinet. The Brigadier was lying in a fold in the hillside with Amin and Taylor outlining the plan for the battle to come. They were both swelteringly overdressed; Amin uniformed and medalled, Taylor in a blindingly white surplice and heavily embroidered clerical stole. Field Marshal and Archbishop.

'Field Marshal Amin will, of course, lead the attack.' Birtwistle had taken the precaution of drawing a diagram on a scrap of paper in case words by themselves failed to penetrate the Field Marshal's consciousness.

Amin nodded his professional judgement. 'Feel marshall up front scare dem cry down they legs I'm tinkin. You tinkin too.'

'Precisely, Mr. President, couldn't have put it better. Or should that be wetter?'

Amin chuckled his rhinoceros chuckle. 'I bin made you better sensoyouma oready Imtinkin.'

'Much better. I'll be having them rolling in the mess when I tell them that in real life you're even funnier than your reputation suggests, President.'

Taylor looked put out at this show of respect.

'But. President Taylor's unparalleled expertise in guerrilla warfare, I'd suggest, makes him ideally suited to command the rearguard. And that would also mean he's in the perfect position to... dissuade anyone who's tempted to desert?'

Taylor's demeanour brightened as he remembered happy days of dissuasion during the long Liberian civil wars when his prayers had been answered and many a deserter had been liberated from the shackles of sin to a better place. Usually with the saintly intervention of a rope and a tree.

Birtwistle explained that he, for his part, would take three men and sabotage the tank. Specialist work for which he'd been intensively trained. They synchronised watches. The Brigadier pointed out to Amin where the big and little hands needed to be before he advanced. Then, having picked three of the dozier looking soldiers, Birtwistle set off past the helicopter pad in the direction of the sunken path called The Side that skirted Jamestown.

***

'No, Minister, casual attire would be *quite* unsuitable. And that *particular* casual attire is an affront to both taste and decency, if I may be so bold.'

'What's the matter with it? Mrs. P. went to great lengths to pick it special. Well, she went to TK Max in Hull, anyroad and she didn't have the Ministerial car that day and if you knew what Mrs. P. thinks about having to go shopping on the bus and getting her hair messed up in the wind you wouldn't be so snooty.'

'What's the matter with it?' Harriet pondered. 'Well, let me see. Shall we start with the lady in a bikini – sorry, almost in a bikini, who graces the back of your shirt. One suspects that, while her all too visible attributes may be testosteronic nirvana for the soldiers who've been posted here a long way from wives and girlfriends, she would have a rather more deleterious effect on the staid ladies of St. Helena whom you'll be addressing after lunch. And I don't think our esteemed passenger would care much for it either.'

Prescott, who'd lost her after 'shirt', tried to look over his shoulder at the offending siren as Harriet glanced out of the cabin porthole and saw the cliffs of Turk's Cap looming into view.

'And then, on the front, there's the shark. Well it's either a shark or the shadow spokesman for health and social security...'

'Now we're getting there.' Prescott gave her a little round of applause.

'Either way it hardly says 'gravitas'. It hardly says 'Minister of the Crown'.'

'There you go, one good punch line and you throw the rest of the act away. Seriousness is your curse, Harriet. Carry on like that in the Working Men's and they'd bring the pies on.'

'Time we were down on deck.' Harry Tinsley put his head round the door. 'Just coming alongside.'

'But the Minister has to change.'

'No time for that. Just get him to throw a jacket over the wildlife park. Anyoff, I've seen him in worse.' He decided best not to go into detail about the string vest and egg stained Y fronts.

Five minutes later, as the Challenger was wound in gently to the quay and the companionway was swung down from the port side rail, Prescott emerged still wearing the offending shirt and shorts but partly covered by a jacket thrown round his shoulders that made him look as if he'd been rescued from a fire in a Caribbean hotel. As he stepped into position between Harriet and Tinsley the two security guards emerged into the sunlight flanking a thin man with an unkempt beard, slightly stooped and dressed in a suit obviously made for someone else. He leaned heavily on what looked like an NHS walking stick and the only animation was in his eyes which darted from face to face. He stopped in front of Prescott and when he looked up from the jaws of the leaping fish to the drooping, fleshy countenance of the fisherman, some spark of recognition flickered.

'Take me to Bush.' The menacing voice from behind the door.

'Eyup.' Said Prescott. Which was one word more than Harriet or Tinsley managed.

***

Radovan Karadzic had been the perfect Ship Day subject. As he strolled up the quay and the anthem blared from the speakers frightening the seagulls, he smiled a far away smile and listened intently to Florence's eulogy, looking deep into her eyes – therapist and patient. On the spur of the moment, he invented a little conceit of a poem which wept for the mountains of Montenegro and welcomed the great leader home to his newly liberated Republica Srpska across the sea. The formalities over, Lieutenant Shaffernacher picked up Karadzic's suitcase and black medical bag and led the way through the crowd towards the Consulate Hotel. By the front steps Robert Mugabe was saying goodbye to Gaddafi but, as the hero of the Bosnian Serbs passed by, they stopped and chatted to him for a few moments. Mugabe slipped him a membership application form for the Presidential Action Committee.

It was as Karadzic turned to mount the steps that the first shot rang out and echoed round the rooftops of Jamestown, accompanied by a strangle of bagpipe drones. Instinctively, all three great leaders crouched and headed for the hotel doorway, the ingrained reaction of men who'd brushed off many an assassination attempt.

In the slow motion moment that followed the first shot, Florence felt herself for bullet holes while registering the line of armed soldiers, Amin skirling at their head, marching clumsily down the ladder. The operator of the dockside crane crashed on the brake leaving the cage carrying Saddam Hussein and his two medical orderlies swinging alarmingly above the quay. Pike dived for cover behind the Saddam statue and the welcoming crowds screamed and scattered. On the bridge of the Bellerophon, Captain Pertwee ordered that the ship's forward guns be trained on the town. He'd always wanted to do that.

Then the shooting started again but this time from the gardens of the public library near the quay where Major Harding's men were dug in behind the garden walls. Their aim was such that the seagulls had more to fear than the rebels, but the distant drones spluttered and some of the men on the ladder fired their guns in the air as they turned and tried to run. In the middle of the melee Bokassa's litter pitched like a gilded fishing boat in heavy seas. Pike, peeping out from behind Saddam's sawn off knees, registered the saintly figure of Charles Taylor bringing up the rear. He stood arms outstretched like the Christ of Rio De Janeiro, except that he had an AK 47 in one hand. But he had no chance to use it because, as Pike watched, a scrambling soldier who'd already thrown his gun away, kicked him in the saintly crotch and Taylor did an impression of Thomas a Beckett's final moments. The deserter trampled over him but only got a couple of steps further up The Ladder when another line of soldiers appeared like the Indians round the canyon rim in all bad cowboy movies. Shwartz and the reserves had let themselves out of the tin sheeted Arrivals Hall, having sweltered there for some hours and now blocked the escape.

It was all over in a matter of minutes. The tank rolled out from behind the post office and its turret swivelled towards the panicking men on The Ladder. At the same time Birtwistle walked out to the centre of the square. The three soldiers who'd been with him had sensibly taken to the hills having been told that Amin planned to serve them up as the victory feast.

Birtwistle tapped the megaphone. 'I'd be most awfully grateful, Mr President – sorry, Mr Presidents, if you'd order your men to put down their weapons.' A clatter of falling weaponry and a saintly groan broke the momentary silence.

'Pamission return him barracks pronto way.' The voice boomed round the square and along the valley. Amin clicked his heels and was back in those happy, carefree days when the officers of the King's Africa Rifles told him when he could shit and when he could shave and which end to use for which.

'Permission granted, Mr. President.'

And to the strains of *I'll take the high road*, Amin's army slouched down The Ladder and a nervous Major Harding led the way across the square in the direction of Jamestown jail.

Birtwistle turned towards the quay as they passed and said into the megaphone 'Carry on Miss Lacey.'

***

Sir Henry watched the little group walk slowly down the companionway in single file. Under his breath he said to Lady Ethne, 'I see the Deputy PM is living up to his reputation. No wonder the country's going down the bloody drain.'

'At least it's going down colourfully. Perhaps we should get you a shirt like that for the next Foreign Office bash. The Foreign Secretary's heart may not survive it,' Ethne murmured through an unbroken smile just before Prescott came within earshot and Harriet bounced into action.

'Sir Henry Jardine, I presume. May I introduce the Deputy

Prime Minister and Minister for Overseas Development.'

'Pleasure,' said Sir Henry, making the word sound like a curse. Harriet ploughed on regardless.

'And this is Mr. Tinsley from the shipping line and we're charged by Her Majesty's Government to deliver our passenger...'

The explosion at the end of the quay sent a cloud of black smoke and a shower of sparks high over the bow of the Challenger. The guards spun round, guns at the ready. Sir Henry ducked and his plumed hat was dislodged onto the concrete, Harry Tinsley looked to see if his ship was still in one piece and the passenger dropped his stick and fell to his knees. Prescott thought the man was trying to make a run for it and reacted by pinning him to the ground with a foot on his neck.

Sixty feet above this little tableau, General Noriega took aim. Another explosion sent a plume of spray sixty feet into the air, this time at the stern of the ship. When it came back to earth it soaked everyone on the quay. In the ensuing confusion, Noriega and his men slipped away through the rocks.

***

'Eleven forty. Almost the moment of truth.' Blair said, checking his watch as he paced the floor in his office in the House of Commons.

'How many times do I have to tell you, Tony. We don't do moments of truth any more.' Alistair Campbell was sitting with his feet up watching a pair of obesities with gargantuan cleavages shouting at each other about the boyfriend who'd done the dirty on both of them and other meanings of life on the Jerry Springer show. 'This is truth, me boy. Anything that gets the audience on its feet baying for blood.'

'Can I just try the speech once more?' He sat at his desk and looked into the camera. The crew from the BBC had gone for a tea break ahead of the live Prime Ministerial broadcast at noon. 'You'll have to do the autocue, Alistair.'

Campbell turned down the volume and rolled the words.

'We live in an increasingly dangerous world and there are times when it seems that governments are powerless to do anything about it...'

'Bit more doom in the delivery, I reckon.'

'We live in an increasingly dangerous *and turbulent* world – that's better isn't it?' Campbell typed the extra words in. 'But today I'm able to make an announcement that shines a ray of light into the darkness and brings a measure of hope rather than despair...I like that bit.'

'I liked it when I wrote it, too.'

'Let's skip on to the end because I want to make sure the tone of that is just right.'

The lines of words whizzed up the screen.

'...We've often been accused in recent months of being America's lapdog. But today's events go to show that the skill of Britain's armed forces combined with the independence and vision of my government have achieved what the superpowers could not.'

'Cracking, if I say so myself,' said Campbell himself.

'I'll just do the very end..... I would also like to make one further announcement. Having set the world on a safer course, I've decided to stand down as.....'

'Quiet.' Campbell ran to the television and turned up the sound.

'We interrupt the Jerry Springer Show for an important newsflash. The Russian Press Agency, Isvestia, has just announced that the leader of al Quaeda, Osama Bin Laden, has been captured.' Blair was still mouthing 'Prime Minister...' as he stared at the screen.

'It's believed British troops may have had some involvement because Isvestia's exclusive pictures, taken on an unidentified dockside, appear to show the British Deputy Prime Minister travelling incognito and restraining the fugitive....'

When the picture appeared on screen of Prescott with teeth gritted and his foot on Bin Laden's neck the cry of 'NO...' from Tony Blair could be heard in the central lobby.

Alistair Campbell's response was quieter. He just said 'Bastard.

Bastard. Bastard.' And then added, 'and we've got just eleven minutes to re-write your speech.'

***

The news, as reported, of course didn't reach the Colony until much later. There it was business as usual. Osama Bin Laden was settled in with his guards in the cave system constructed at the deepest part of the barred tunnel in the cliff.

'Rather more homely than the ones at Bora Bora, I'm sure.' Said Lady Ethne encouragingly as she wandered from room to room, adjusting this piece of furniture and that. 'Such efficient use of space. And so cool, Mr. Laden.'

But the finer points of interior design and air conditioning appeared to pass the new resident by.

'Take me to Bush' was all he would say.

'One must be so, so careful not to allow obsessions to run away with one's life.' Lady Jardine urged gently. 'Most unhealthy. Never know where it will end. I'll send across my beginner's guide to Pilates for Health. Healthy mind, healthy body, Mr. Laden. And who knows what good things you could achieve.'

The Challenger's deck cranes swiftly unloaded the large crates of security cargo which were also stored away in the tunnel. Harry Tinsley joked, briefly, with John Prescott about how his ability to put his foot in it had, for once, paid off. As soon as Tinsley was back on board, the Challenger sailed, and Sir Henry and Lady Jardine had the pleasure of the Deputy Prime Minister's abundance of tasteless jokes all the way back to Jamestown. After such an exciting morning no amount of tutting from Harriet could stop him.

"And have you heard the one about the poodle that bit his master?" Prescott raised an eyebrow in Harriet's direction. "You know, I've just forgotten the punch line to that one. Remind me, Harriet. Isn't that the one I overhead you telling Harry Tinsley?'

For once Harriet didn't tut.

In Jamestown things had settled down, too. Saddam Hussein had been transferred from his dangling cage to the padded cell in the island hospital which had been prettily decorated with pictures of his palaces in Baghdad. Gadaffi had sailed on the Bellerophon after a minor delay caused by the problem of getting his favourite camel aboard. Jamestown prison was the busiest it had been in years with all five cells full to bursting and a barrage of complaints from the island's drunks who couldn't find space to sleep off their hangovers.

Presidents Amin and Taylor got a standing ovation from the Presidential Action Committee when Birtwistle took them for afternoon tea in the Consulate Hotel. Bokassa's litter was carried shoulder high round the palm court and he blessed everyone with his faintly flashing neon crucifix.

In the British Embassy Pike and Momo were helping themselves to large measures of the Ambassador's scotch in the butler's pantry and in the basement of the American Embassy, Donald Reeves, oblivious to the real hostilities in Jamestown that morning, had moved on to the first Gulf War.

Three floors up, Mrs. Reeves, Florence and Noriega were celebrating as the General passed round the photographs he'd sent by satellite phone to Isvestia. They laughed at the thought of the tidal waves of diplomatic excrement that would already be washing back and forth across the Atlantic.

Theo Bloor could be found gibbering at his usual table in the White Horse, dreaming of Ahna and planning to make a start any day now on the sculpture which the Deputy Prime Minister was supposed to be unveiling the following morning.

In the Cable and Wireless monitoring station Hanrahan had picked up the signal from the illicit satellite phone but couldn't read its encrypted message. He'd sent the code red to Reeves who was still listed as duty officer and got a message back proclaiming that Kuwait was free.

Eight thousand miles to the north Gordon Brown was throwing a party.

Twelve thousand miles to the north west, George Bush wasn't.

EPILOGUE

It was Ship Day. On the quay the American Marines band was briskly running through the National Anthems and the British Honour Guard was as woeful as it had ever been. Florence Lacey was doing a final check of the new protocols which had been established when the Joint Powers decided all future Ship Days should be organised by the British and the Americans in partnership.

'It'll never bloody work,' had been Sir Henry Jardine's predictable response when he first heard the news, but today he'd mellowed. As Momo drove the ancient Rolls Royce out of the Embassy compound and slowly down Main Street towards the quay, Sir Henry and Lady Ethne happily chatted about Ship Days past and the excitements of the day to come.

Ethne gave one of her off-duty, horsy laughs which she saved for moments when the two of them were on their own. 'I think they're going to look like Tweedledum and Tweedledee, both in their strait jackets.'

'At least Saddam's got virgins to look forward to. Best Reeves can hope for is a nurse who keeps her needles sharp.'

'Bit of a turn up the old Mrs. Reeves becoming the new Mrs. Pike, though.'

'Flavour of the month. Cementing Anglo American relations, Ethne. I'm surprised you didn't know. They've been cementing for months. Cementing like Balfour Beattie's rabbits.'

'I think I get the point, Henry.'

'Just surprised you didn't know they were at it. That's all.'

Momo smiled.

'But I bet *you* didn't know..' said Ethne, slightly miffed. '..that Miss Lacey has taken up with that nice Mr. Hanrahan.'

'Fraid I did. French Consul rang to complain about goings on at Boney's tomb. I never realised, but apparently they're so proud of the bloody place that they've got it covered with a security camera from Longwood. Course being French he didn't mind about the sex. It was the sun tan cream that was spoiling the bloody patina.'

Good job Henry's a technophobe, thought Ethne, glancing at Momo in the driver's mirror. But Henry didn't notice because he was looking out of the window at Bloor, already staggering, at eleven in the morning, from the tin shed behind the post office where he now lived and didn't work. 'Riff raff.' Henry growled. 'Give me an honest dictator any day.' And he waved cheerily at President Aristide who'd looked up from the little group of spares he was teaching in the shade of a Eucalyptus tree on Main Street and waved back.

At the pier head the car pulled up alongside Birtwistle who was surrounded by heaps of baggage waiting to be loaded onto the ship.

'Morning, Ambassador, Lady Jardine, and a fine one it is, too. Ready for the off?'

'As we'll ever be.' Said Henry.

'And we're so pleased you've agreed to come with us.' Ethne lightly touched Birtwistle on the sleeve. 'With you as our military attaché and of course Henry's acknowledged love of the American way I'm sure the Washington Embassy is going to be frightfully exciting.'

'I'm sure the White House and the Pentagon have no idea what's about to hit them.' Birtwistle chuckled at the thought of Sir Henry in all his glory.

'Can't imagine what you mean, Brigadier.' Sir Henry attempted an angelic smile and failed.

A Land Rover arrived from the hospital and a squad of medical orderlies unloaded Saddam Hussein and a wildly staring Donald Reeves. The band played a medley of National Anthems as the patients were gently manoeuvred down the quay. Reeves occasionally surfaced from the sea of chemical tranquillity in which he was swimming and like a sad old man berating the rush hour crowd, shouted dire warnings of nuclear tests in North Korea, terrorist attacks in Texas and impending defeat in Vietnam. All that was missing was the Prepare to Meet Thy God placard. Saddam Hussein, in contrast, just smiled and gently nodded, first to one side then the other, as he greeted his adoring people.

'Don't know how he got away with it for so long,' said Sir Henry. 'He always was a bloody awful actor.'

'Is that Saddam or Reeves you're talking about?' Ethne's little joke.

Pike strode about, sorting out this and that. He'd smartened up. He looked quite the master of ceremonies. Lady Ethne thought Mrs. Reeves must have been taking him in hand. The faintest hint of a smile appeared when she thought that behind every great man is a woman wearing a set of cinema curtains.

'And your position will be somewhere here, Mr. Ambassador.' Pike showed the Colony's new American representative to his place on the red carpet.

'And how long's this baloney going to take?' Ambassador Rumsfeld didn't suffer fools gladly and Pike's association with the British Diplomatic Service put him squarely in that category. 'I've got proper work to do and playing pass the parcel with a bunch of fucking loony toons aint proper work in my book.'

'Oh, no longer than about half an hour if everything goes according to plan.'

'It doesn't look very planned to me.' Rumsfeld's sadly accusing look was magnified by his rimless spectacles as he scanned the scene of confusion around him.

'Amazing how quickly it all comes together once we spot the ship rounding the point,' Mr. Ambassador.

'When I was in the US Navy, Mr. Pike, ships rounded points at the point in time they were supposed to round points.'

'We do know that Northumberland's due to drop anchor in..' Pike consulted his watch. '…in twenty minutes time.'

Rumsfeld adjusted his shoulders in the expensive suit he managed to make look cheap and became almost poetic in his disdain.

'Mr. Pike, as I've said before.

As we know, There are known knowns. There are things we know we know. We also know There are known unknowns. That is to say We know there are some things We do not know. But there are also unknown unknowns, The ones we don't know We don't know.
And the arrival of the Northumberland
Seems to me
To fall into
That category.'

'Still talking bollocks, then Rummy. Anyoff, good to see some things never change even after the tides of ingratitude have started to run. Mugabe was just saying that yesterday. Canny bloke, Robert. Nowhere near as bad as he's painted.' Ambassador Prescott, crammed into a frock coat and plumed hat was red in the face. He looked like a fat, flightless bird.

'Johnny! Thank the Almighty there's somebody here tells it like it is,' said Rumsfeld turning his back on Pike and pumping Prescott's hand. 'Somebody who speaks my language.'

'How's Joyce?'

'How the hell would you be if you'd had to listen to me for 56 years?'

'When you see what it's done to Dubya you've got a point, Donny.'

'Can't blame me for that. There's things you know, Johnny, and things you don't. And there's things you should know and things you shouldn't. And one of the things you should know, Johnny, is that you don't stick your chewing gum up yer backside like peppermint suppositories.'

Even Prescott, used as he was to the reinvention of language, looked puzzled for a moment as he waited for the explanation that never came. Then he shrugged.

'Never had that problem myself, Rummy, Couldn't have reached if I'd wanted. Anyroad, Pauline's looking forward to seeing Joyce at the social up the Consulate tonight. Says that Saddam Hussein lookalike on this week does a great act. Specially when he does the shopping list in Saddam style and sings some of his speeches to the music from Annie Get Your Gun. Brought the house down. Pauline laughed so much she almost messed up her hair.'

'Great idea of yours, John, the Presidential Working Men's Club. Gives them something sensible to complain about.'

'Aye, price of ale and gristle in the pies is a grand leveller. Only one I feel sorry for is Mengiwhatsistu, him what talks like a dalek. Copped for club secretary and world over everybody hates the club secretary.'

'Least for the first time in their miserable lives they've been called working men, John. Some people know they are and some people don't know they're not; some people don't know they don't know they're not but these ones have been told they are. Best compliment they've ever been paid, John.'

'Learned that trick working with the unions at British Leyland. Most of them didn't know they didn't know bugger all as well.'

Pike coughed, somewhere behind Prescott's shoulder. 'Sorry to interrupt, sir, but just thought you should know Northumberland has dropped anchor.'

'Not before time and this is not before time,' said Rumsfeld decisively.

The dockside crane clattered into life and the cage was swung ashore. The strains of an anthem Rumsfeld didn't immediately recognise rose on the still air and Captain Macdiarmid walked slowly forward with his passenger. Under the banner Welcome Home President for Life and Saviour of Our Nation a little cheer rippled through the crowd. The delegation from the Working Men's waved their flags and Florence Lacey pulled the cord and unveiled the bronze statue that had been brought from Turk's Cap that morning. It portrayed a slight figure with prominent ears striking a Churchillian pose, metal hands clutching metal lapels.

As the sheet fell away the passenger looked up and smiled. Prescott's red face broke into a wide grin.

'Tony.'

***

Ten miles away, across the island, Osama Bin Laden was taking his morning walk through the tunnel system at Turk's Cap. He stopped for a while, as he always did, at the barred gates and looked out over the quay to the rolling Atlantic. On his way back to his cave he paused at the stack of crates stored in the tunnel. One of the wooden boxes had been damaged and he prised up a corner of the splintered lid. Inside in the darkness he saw a block of pink stone and the word that each night rose, unbidden, in his dreams. BUSH.

He shouted a phrase in Arabic which, roughly translated, meant 'The bastards. They got to him before I did.'

Eight thousand miles to the north, at Heathrow Airport, Prime Minister Brown stepped briskly along the red carpet to the steps of Airforce One to welcome President Clinton on her first official visit to her staunchest ally.

Twelve miles to the east, at a foundry in Bermondsey, workmen were putting the finishing touches to a fine, big statue. Rumour had it that it was destined for the empty plinth in Trafalgar Square, close by the Ugandan embassy. It showed a larger than life figure in full highland dress playing the bagpipes. His left foot rested on the neck of a vanquished Lion. Beneath it a small plaque carried the single word – Brown.